All Moms
Go to Heaven

All Moms Go to Heaven

REFLECTIONS BY

Dean Hughes

—⟨ ✳ ⟩—

DESERET
BOOK

SALT LAKE CITY, UTAH

In memory of my mother,
Lorraine Pierce Hughes

Library of Congress Cataloging-in-Publication Data

Hughes, Dean, 1943–
    All moms go to heaven / Dean Hughes.
        p.   cm.
    ISBN 1-59038-424-5 (pbk.)
    1. Motherhood. 2. Fatherhood. 3. Child rearing. I. Title.
    HQ759.H844 2005
    306.874'3—dc22

                                    2004025650

Printed in the United States of America   54459
Malloy Lithographing, Inc., Ann Arbor, MI

10   9   8   7   6   5   4

Contents

—◄ ✽ ►—

I Was a Mother

——< ✳ >——

Some might wonder whether a man really knows much about motherhood. But I can talk with a certain degree of authority. After all, I was once a mother myself.

Okay, so I didn't actually give birth to a baby—although I would have been willing had the opportunity come up—but I was a stay-at-home "person" for an entire summer when my kids were five, three, and three months old, and at the same time I tended two other children, ages nine and seven. I've been there!

This all happened in 1973, just after I had finished my first year of teaching. I was an assistant professor of English, bringing in the princely sum of $12,100 a year. The trouble was, I was paid only for the nine months I taught, and Kathy and I found it impossible (for some reason) to save enough money to get us through the summer. When Kathy was offered a fellowship to work on her master's degree in a new field in special education called "Learning

Disabilities"—and even granted a stipend for living costs—the opportunity was just too good to pass up. We did a lot of thinking and praying about the situation and decided that Kathy was not only receiving a wonderful blessing but that I, too, would have a rich and rewarding experience. I would be able to grow closer to my children—and truly bond with them. I would also (this was my thought, not Kathy's, as I recall) be able to have a laid-back summer with time to read and prepare for my fall classes. After years of pressure in graduate school, followed by a tension-filled year of teaching and research, I thought it sounded fun to have time to play with my wonderful little kids and, for once in my life, experience some downtime.

If this sounds a little too much like the plot to *The Perfect Storm,* you haven't heard anything yet. We realized, for one thing, that the small stipend Kathy would receive would never be enough to keep us going for the entire summer, and yet it was virtually impossible for a professor to find summer work in the small Missouri town where we lived. But Kathy was able to find an evening job at the local TG & Y variety store. This was another blessing, we told ourselves. True, she would be gone pretty much all day on weekdays and all evening four nights of the week, but we would be able to put food on our table. Then serendipity struck again. I found a source for a little more income myself. A woman who taught in the English Department, a friend of mine, was teaching that summer but didn't want to leave her nine and seven-year-old daughters alone. I offered to look after them, and she said she would pay me!

Hey, I'm no fool. I saw the opportunity. Young girls love babies.

I would "tend" the two girls, but in truth, they would play with my kids, feed my baby, change his diapers, and generally add to the level of fun around the house. Meanwhile, I would be able to get all the more study and research done. It's amazing how things fall together sometimes. I was a happy man.

Okay. I know what you're thinking. I was naïve. I was living in a fool's paradise. But actually, things worked out exactly as I planned. The girls, guided by their mother, came with little books and paper dolls so they could have fun with my kids. They read stories to them, played games, and clearly enjoyed the experience. That lasted, as I recall, the better part of the first morning. I don't think the initial battle was engaged until afternoon. But after that, it was open war!

As it turned out, these girls were nice, but they liked to read and watch TV, and they were accustomed to a quiet life together. It was one thing to read a story or play paper dolls for an hour or two, but after that they wanted their own time and their own TV shows, and two *little* kids (not to mention a crying baby) soon became *bothers* to them. Before the week was out, my children were *the enemy*.

No one got seriously hurt. Mostly I heard threats, warnings, screams of rage, and doors slamming (as the girls tried to find places to hide away). There was also only one TV in the house, and the big kids never stopped fighting with the little kids about what they wanted to watch. I'll even admit that before the summer was over I got into that argument myself at times (after all, moms have needs, too).

Well, okay, here's the point. I had my eyes *opened* that summer.

Opened *wide*. I can now honestly say that I've been there, done that, and have the scars to prove it. And I'll tell you this: men just don't understand what we mothers go through.

I didn't read that summer. Not *anything*. I didn't even get to the newspaper. If you're a mom you understand that, of course, but as the realization set in on me, I'll admit right now, I began to suffer symptoms of depression. I got so I didn't care much what I looked like. Who would see me anyway? And I snacked way too much. It was almost the only thing I had to look forward to—a little chocolate to comfort me when the stress got too great. And stress was a way of life. I'm the kind of person who likes to focus on a task, follow it through, get it finished, and move on. I get a great deal done, and it's because I get after a job and conclude it. But there's no finishing anything in the child-care, home-care business. When I think of that summer, I still get a mental picture of confusion and chaos, as though a hurricane had blown the whole time. I hear noise, see toys scattered everywhere, smell sour milk, and feel Robert, our baby boy, squirm in my grasp as I try to pin him into his diapers.

Yes, that's right. You young mothers don't know what we used to go through. I was using cloth diapers that summer, the kind you fold yourself. Robert was six months old by the end of the summer, and the older he got, the harder he fought against being held down long enough for a diaper change. And there were no sticky little plastic strips to slap down quickly on those old diapers. There were big, dangerous pins—dangerous to the baby, of course, but much more likely to end up sticking me in the thumb. (The potential for tetanus was always on my mind.)

Now let me make one thing perfectly clear (as President Nixon liked to say): I had started changing our kids' diapers right from the beginning. I had a very good attitude about that sort of thing. I wanted to be involved with my kids. I wanted to be a nurturer. The women's movement of the late sixties had raised my consciousness, and I wanted to be one of the new, sensitive fathers who wasn't afraid to show love to his kids. I had male friends who refused to change diapers, and I gave them a bad time about that. My favorite line was, "You go out and work on your car and get grease all over your hands, and you don't mind that at all. Well, there's nothing in a baby's diaper that won't wash off a lot more easily than that grease."

So I was enlightened and experienced. But changing a diaper back in those days was only the beginning. Once the new diaper was on, and the rubber pants were pulled over the diaper (as the baby continued to squirm), the real work began. First, I had to dip the diaper in our toilet (there was only one in our little house, which was a constant problem) and wring it out. Then I would hold my breath, open the diaper pail, and dump the thing in. You may not realize that urine, when it ages, turns to ammonia, and ammonia is sometimes used to wake up a battered boxer or a stunned football player. (It's a historical fact that sailors used to save urine and scrub the decks of ships with it.) So the act of dropping the diaper in the pail was always like a shot to the head with a fist. And it was important not to let those diapers stew too long. The ammonia could build up and cause rash problems for the baby.

The next step, of course, was to wash those diapers, but it is almost unbelievable the number a baby can use up. I would fold two together, just to catch all the wet dear little Robert could produce. So it was into the washing machine with the diapers, but when they came out, I didn't put them in the dryer. We had a dryer, but it was ghastly slow, and we didn't want to use too much electricity. (Besides, Kathy told me the sunshine would kill off the ammonia.) So I would hang out the diapers on the clothesline in the backyard. After the diapers dried in the air, I would haul them back in, and the folding and re-wetting cycle would start once again.

Okay, that sounds like work. But I've described all this as though I were a washerwoman, and that's all I had to do all day. The problem is, first, that while a mom is changing the diaper, older kids see their opportunity. The main goal of Tommy, at five, and Amy, at three, was to look for new adventures. After all, kids need to learn. That's their job.

Tommy would sense that I was occupied (he could feel it through the walls) and decide it was a good time to dive off the back of the couch on his head (just to see how that might feel). Or Amy would decide that she wanted to try out her *actual* mother's bath powder. So sometimes, just as I was wrestling with Robert and the pins, I would hear screams from the living room, or worse, I would hear nothing at all. A mom soon learns that silence is the most dangerous sound in a house.

I would pick up Robert and rush out to do reconnaissance, repair, or first aid, and sometimes, in my haste, I would leave the "used" diaper on the family room floor. I have stories about forgotten diapers that you really don't want to hear. Experienced mothers, at least from the cloth-diaper era, know what I'm talking about. (I'm remembering one story right now that's related, in its own strange way. I killed a cockroach one day and walked away to get a Kleenex to clean it up with. When I got back, the roach was gone. I looked at Robert, who seemed quite satisfied with himself. Then I noticed a cockroach leg hanging from his lip.)

More often, however, I at least got as far as the toilet, and I would drop the diaper in. But when some other emergency or pressing need came ("Daddy, I'm firsty." Kids are *always* firsty.), I would not rinse the diaper out immediately. The problem is, children have a way of knowing these things, and they have a killer's instinct. About three times out of ten, they would make me pay for my mistake. They would wander in and flush the toilet and, if I was lucky, it only overflowed, and the diaper didn't go down so deep that I had to call a plumber.

But let's go back to that crucial time when the diaper has been washed and needs to make its way outside to the clothesline. The trouble is, the kids are in the house. So I would have two choices: bring Tommy and Amy out with me and tell them to play in the yard, and maybe set the baby on a blanket, *or* take a chance. Live dangerously. I could ask the older girls to help, then run outside and try to hang the wash quickly while the kids were watching *Sesame Street* or some such thing. This method sounds acceptable, but three minutes alone—even with theoretical supervision—is a long time, and if something happens to the little dears, the police will want to know where you were.

I never found a good answer to these problems. It's now called multitasking, and mothers are said to be very good at it. But maybe I mentioned before, I'm a person who likes to focus on a job and get it done. Living in a five-ring circus was absolutely shattering to me. The older girls weren't much of a problem if left to themselves (although they did complain of boredom quite often), but they never stopped arguing with the little kids or complaining to me about them. The other three all wanted something from me—and all at the same time.

Little Amy would still not be dressed an hour after Kathy had left for the day, and the baby would be crying for no reason whatsoever, and Tommy would want me to help him build a house out of Lincoln Logs (even though he would lose interest soon after I started). The arguments never ended over who had hit whom first, and who had called whom a poopy face. Everything was always happening at once, and I never stopped trying to get it all under control.

And then there were the meals to prepare. In a way, I didn't have it so tough because Kathy was always home in the morning and would prepare breakfast, but in the midst of everything going on after she left, it was surprisingly difficult to get those dishes washed, or at least cleared off to the sink. (We had no dishwasher to hide dishes away in.) Amazingly, time had a way of moving in opposite directions. On the one hand, the days seemed tediously long; on the other, mealtimes came every few minutes.

The kids would show no interest at all in eating while at the table, and I would try all kinds of airplane tricks, begging, etc., to get them to eat a little, but a few minutes after a meal they were not only firsty but also hungwy. A couple of minutes after that, it seemed, lunchtime would be upon us. I started the summer with a lot of PB & J, but the older girls began to complain, so I had to come up with bologna sandwiches or tuna fish, or some such thing, and invariably a majority didn't like whatever it was. So I'd cajole them into eating as best I could—sometimes dealing with someone choking on the peanut butter—and then they all were hungwy again.

Diapers and dishes (sorry to put those words together) were only two of the jobs I faced with shocking frequency. I really wanted Kathy to come home to a clean house (so she wouldn't think I was taking it easy all day), and that's why I always meant to make the beds, but I often found little opportunity to get to such things. More than anything, though, I suffered from the never-ending job of controlling the clutter.

Kids don't know how to get a toy out. They know how to dump toy boxes upside down and then sort through the mess for something to play with (often finding nothing and complaining about it). And toys always seem to come in sets of a million pieces. It's one thing to get out a truck or a doll, but there were always sets of blocks, Tinker Toys, or Lincoln Logs. Or there were games with lots of pieces, which were more fun to dump into a bucket and then onto the floor than to use for their actual purpose. So I would always have marbles and Old Maid cards, dice, and a hundred other things scattered everywhere—sometimes dangerously close to the baby. Potato chips, carrot sticks, and bread crusts (spread with peanut butter) had a way of getting mixed in.

Here was my solution. I would let the kids dump everything out, leave it all out, and then, when they finally went to bed at night (and I'll get to that ordeal later), even though I was exhausted, I would pick up everything, maybe run a vacuum over the floor, and Kathy would be pleased to see a clean house when she got home on those late evenings. But there was a problem with that, too. Kathy would say, "I hope you're teaching the kids to take care of their toys. If you pick everything up for them, they won't learn a thing." Of course, I didn't dare say, "Oh, yeah? Do you have any idea what I've been through here today?"

Kathy's role that summer was to make sure I understood the importance of guilt in a mother's life. My motivation was to bring some semblance of order to the house, so I wouldn't start the next day in chaos. But according to Kathy's point of view, I was supposed to be training these kids. They needed to understand that they had chores, even at their age, and . . . you know . . . all that stuff. So what was I to do?

I had to choose between efficiency and remorse. It's just so much easier to put toys away than it is to teach children to do it themselves. Hours can go by as you plead, explain, threaten, offer "incentives," and finally blow your top. But if I went ahead and did it myself, Kathy might question me, and I might have to rat on myself. If she didn't ask, I had to wonder whether my kids were going to grow up to be irresponsible creeps.

In the heat of the action, I didn't much care about such

abstractions, but once the kids were finally in bed, I would ask myself what I was doing to them. I shouldn't have gotten so upset about certain things; I should have been a lot more firm about others. Robert needed more attention and affection. And what would Kathy say if she knew I let the whole crew eat those Oreos when they never did eat their carrot sticks (which I had so firmly required as prerequisite)? All three of my kids were probably heading for disease (not enough veggies) and jail (not enough discipline). Besides that, I was messing up my friend's kids while I was messing up my own.

But I'm ahead of myself. I talked about kids going to bed. At the end of a monstrously long day, the hardest job anyone ever invented is the simple act of getting kids to go to bed. Amy, when younger, had not been so bad. She had loved her binkie and her blanket, and she would often settle down peacefully. But then Kathy decided she was too old for a pacifier and that decision ruined my life. The first night without her pacifier, Amy sat on her bed and cried for something like thirty-six hours. Amy could get an idea in her head and cling to it longer than any child I've ever known. Stubborn is for beginners. Amy was passionate, committed, and entirely unreasonable once she thought up something she wanted. And if she wanted her binkie, her childish, little habit was not going to be expunged in a night or two. I still have recurring nightmares of her terrifying breath stoppages, between screams, and of those crushingly disappointing moments when she would almost give up, begin to quiet—then recognize her own weakness and begin to scream again with renewed power.

But Tommy, in some ways, was worse. The boy hated going to bed more than anything I could ask of him. He has remained that way all his life, and now in his thirties, he's still a night owl. He would run through all the "I need a drink of water," "Read me a story" routine, and then he would just keep bouncing back up like a rubber ball. I would bribe him, talk to him, soothe him, get him in bed, tuck him in, suggest that the bedbugs not bite him, and walk out the door, and he would be right behind me. All I wanted was *one hour* of peace before Kathy got home—one hour to watch TV perhaps, since my mind was way too tired to read anything that had literary merit—but Tommy would fight the system in every way he could. He would be quiet for five minutes and I would begin to smile, and then, there he was, asking for something, or I would hear him in his room, out of bed again.

And remember, Tommy and Amy were performing these acts of defiance simultaneously, and the baby was often cranky at the same time. He would cry for sheer expressiveness. I would change his diaper, feed him, rock him, and put him down, and maybe he would hear his sister, or maybe he would model on his brother—I don't know—but suddenly he would start in all over again.

Of all the challenges that summer, the worst was getting our three kids down and asleep without losing my mind or my temper or both. About the time I would finally get the job done, Kathy would walk through the door, and I would try to explain what I had been going through. I don't mean to be too critical of her, but I do have to say, she didn't show nearly as much empathy and under-standing as I thought I deserved. First, she would remind me that she knew all about that stuff, and then there was always the "I've had a hard day myself" line.

Oh, right. Like I hadn't been out there going to college and working part-time all my life? That kind of life is a vacation compared to being home with a bunch of kids—and of all people, *she* ought to know it.

All I wanted from Kathy at that point was a minute or two of her time. I wanted to hear what adults, out there in the real world, talked about. I wanted to tell her some of my trials, seek a little advice, maybe even sob on her shoulder for a minute or two. But she was tired. *Tired?* What did she think *I* was? And she still needed to read a chapter for one of her classes.

(See, there's proof! She could actually still read at that point. My mind was fried.)

I hate to say this, but people who spend their lives away from home all day really don't understand what it's like to be a mother. All I wanted was to say something in a sentence with a few two-syllable words. I wanted to express an opinion that didn't start with, "Tommy, if you do that again . . ." I wanted to find out whether anything had happened in the world that day. (If a UFO had landed in Washington and absconded with President Nixon, how would I know?) And I wanted someone to listen to me. If I told Kathy that the kids had cut a big gash in our kitchen table with a screwdriver, she would want to know how they got hold of the screwdriver. Or if I told her I was afraid that I was in need of counseling and drugs, she would say something like, "It's only three months, Dean. I have them all the time."

That's the kind of insensitivity I have a lot of trouble with. Forever is forever, whether it's three months of forever or twenty years of it. And besides, I *knew* it was only three months. She didn't have to tell me what I knew. All I wanted was to get a few things off my chest, not a "you can do it" speech. Sometimes a person just needs to be understood—you know, just get it all out. He doesn't need to be "instructed" at a time like that.

The truth is, though, I was losing the power of speech. I'm not sure I could have explained my feelings if Kathy had wanted to hear it all. After you've talked to young children for twenty-five straight hours in a day, normal usage begins to atrophy. When you've said, "I know, honey, just a minute" twelve times in a row, only to hear, "No, Daddy. Wight now!" in response, you start saying strange things: "Daddy can't come wight now. Baby Wob will cwy. He needs his baba."

To which Amy replies, "I don't ca'e. Baby Wob's *stubid*."

And then, if a mother is not *really* careful, the argument can begin. "No, *you* the one being stubid, not Wob."

"No, *you* stubid, Daddy."

"Not as stubid as *you*."

About then it's time to count the days that remain in your ninety-day hitch.

You know you're losing it when you have memorized all the little songs on *Sesame Street* and when Mr. Rogers starts to seem like a regular guy. In fact, it was out of that need for adult information, for actual thought, that I got hooked on daytime TV. No, not soaps! I wouldn't go that far. But remember, it was 1973, and that was the summer of the Watergate hearings. In those days there were no car-toon or Disney channels. Children's programming only existed for a while in the morning and then again later in the afternoon. In between, I could listen to—if not really watch—the unfolding of the Watergate drama. The most exciting day of the summer was when Alexander Butterfield revealed that Nixon had made tapes of his White House conversations. That was big stuff, and I would have called a friend to talk it over if my friends hadn't been doing nor-mal things, like going to work. (Sometimes I took my children to a park that summer, but I was never well accepted by the female moms—at least not enough that I could have called one of them.)

The Watergate hearings did give me a little something to look forward to each day. The only problem was, just when the debate would get intense, it would be time for one of those children's pro-grams. Of course, the little kids couldn't tell time, but if they found out the program was over, and they'd missed it, I had *trouble* on my hands. Besides, the older girls would have gladly watched reruns of *Beverly Hillbillies* and *My Three Sons* all day. So they were furious that I would watch a bunch of old men who did nothing but argue.

TV was a problem all summer, and that gets back to my guilt. I really knew that I should be reading to the kids, providing creative projects for them, stimulating their minds, getting them outside for wholesome exercise—but all those things required planning and creativity, and how do you pull that stuff off when the baby needs a bottle? I would have had to coordinate the activities of five kids, nine through zero, and there was no hope of that. So it was just a whole lot easier to let everyone watch television as many hours as humanly possible.

Amy would sit on her little chair and stare at the television as long as kids' shows were on, and Tommy liked most of the same shows. It was like looking a gift horse in the mouth (whatever that means) not to let electric entertainment help me out, but I strongly suspected that if any of my kids ever ended up in prison, someone would finally trace the problem back to TV and then straight on to me. Kathy would remind me that we had to limit the number of hours they watched—and maybe keep it down to some ridiculous number, like two—and I would nod and agree, but almost every day I would let temptation have its way. Cookies, TV, no exercise: I was polluting my own kids, and I didn't have the willpower to stop.

So every now and then I would decide it was time to make a better effort. I would search my brain for an idea and then announce, "Kids, I think we've been watching a little too much TV. Today we're going to read a story together and then—guess what?— act it out. Wow! It's going to be great. Come on, girls, you can help."

Have you ever tried to reason with a child? Kids like to ask "Why?" about everything, or they respond with *non sequitur* arguments: "It's *my* show, Daddy."

"I know, honey. But you don't have to watch it *every* day. Today we're going to—"

"It's my *show*, Daddy."

"I know. But won't it be fun to read a book together and then put on a little play?"

"Pways are *stubid*."

"They are not."

"Are too."

"Are not."

"You're *stubid*, Daddy."

"Oh, sure. You don't even know what a pway is, and you're the one calling it *stubid*. How's that for *stubid*?"

"I know what a pway is, and it's *stubid*."

"What is a pway then?"

"It's *nuffin*."

"What? What's that supposed to mean?"

"It means it's *stubid*."

"That's the most ridiculous logic I've ever heard. You're making up your mind, and you don't know what I'm even talking about. I'm going to put on a pway all by myself. And you kids don't get to help me."

But a dramatic walk from the room doesn't work.

Okay. I made up that conversation. I don't remember the real arguments, but I know they were at least that "stubid." And I remember the feeling that some sort of mush was taking over my cranium, filling it up. After a while you begin to wonder whether you will ever be normal again. A three-year-old has taken you on verbally and whupped you, and you're in the next room muttering, "Yeah, well, you're not so smart. I'm a *professor*, I want you to know. I get paid to tell people . . . stuff."

The worst single disappointment in raising kids is holding on and holding on, trying to be patient, trying to explain, trying to encourage, trying to reprimand with love, and then, finally, losing your temper. "I told you, *just a minute*," I would finally bellow, and look down to see a lip begin to quiver. President McKay used to say there was never a reason for parents to raise their voices. I believed that—still do—but there I would be, shouting at a kid because she had just smeared peanut butter on the bathroom doorknob, or because he had asked you for the thirty-second time, "Why can't I go outside?" And suddenly you're yelling, "*Because I said so.*" And then you see his little face go limp and his bottom lip stick out, and you drop down and take him in your arms and tell him you're sorry. But you know you've blown it *one more time.*

If things go the usual way, after you do something like that, you give in to something you were trying to be firm about, and you feel guilty about that, so you end up at the end of the day trying to remember one thing you did right. The worst is when your babies finally go to sleep, and you go in to check on them, pull their blankets up around their pretty little faces, and vow to love them the next day—just love them. And then morning comes, with another breakfast, more "firstiness," more toys all over, more arguments, with the baby crying in the middle of it all, and those diapers not dry even though he needs one right now.

In all seriousness, I got depressed that summer. I've exaggerated some of these things, for fun, but I did struggle with myself. I didn't go into a clinical depression; I knew the summer would end, eventually. But I was often disappointed with myself for my impatience and crankiness, and for my failure to teach the kids what I wanted them to learn. But the worst thing—the thing that kept me unhappy—was getting up in the morning and thinking, "This day will be just like yesterday and tomorrow." My only goal each day was to get back to where I started in the morning. The house was always messier and dirtier than I wanted, and so were the kids. (I haven't said anything about giving baths, but that was another ordeal I won't go into right now.)

I had spent my whole life feeling that a good day was one in which I either got a lot done or indulged myself a little by reading or traveling or having a rich and interesting conversation. I felt constantly as though I needed to get *my* work done, but there was never an end to keeping up with the immediate, constant needs of the children. And yet, I knew how important it was to treat them fairly and patiently, and how crucial my actions could be in their lives. I felt guilty virtually every day. It always seemed that I was letting them—and their "permanent mother"—down.

Worth the Work?

—< ✳ >—

The summer of 1973 was unquestionably the hardest of my life. I am not kidding. There is no tongue in my cheek when I say that. I had spent some summers out in the sun, working on construction, but that was an eight-hour job, so it hardly compared. Since then I've spent many summers teaching or sitting at a computer all day, writing. That's paradise by comparison. All the same, I do have some great memories of my experience with my kids, and it wouldn't be fair not to mention some of those.

I said that bath time was always crazy—and wet—but one of my favorite memories from that summer has to do with bath time. Tommy and Amy hated to get into the tub and then didn't want to get out. (Some things are universal.) I could let them play and splash for quite some time, and mostly, I only had to stay close so no one got hurt and no floods occurred. But Robert needed to be bathed. I would hold him by his little shoulder, with my own arm across his chest (I learned that hold in one of those prenatal classes Kathy and I took before Tommy was born). Robert loved the water and liked to splash, too. He was a sturdy little guy (we started calling him "Chunky Beef" not long after that), but he was soft, too, in the way that only a baby can be soft. I remember lifting him from the tub and wrapping him in a big towel and carrying him out to put his diaper on. But he loved to kick and be free. (I'm convinced that every child—and probably every human—would really rather be naked.) So I would let him enjoy his nakedness sometimes, when other demands didn't call me. (That, of course, is dangerous business with a baby boy, and I took more than one shot in the eye.)

What I remember, though, is his joy, and I remember his infant softness, his babbling, and his innocence. I have a picture in my mind of his wonderful smile.

I had no idea, then, that time would go so fast, but it did. Rob, as we call him now, is an attorney in Salt Lake City, and he has his own little boy. His son, Billy, is two. He's not as chunky as Rob was, and he looks a lot like his pretty mom, but there are moments when Billy smiles and I see baby Robert all over again. Billy is a great kid who talks more than any other two-year-old I've ever known— except for his father, when he was the same age.

Once, when Robert was four, our family took a trip to the Ozarks in southern Missouri. Tommy was nine by then and hadn't become Tom yet. He was a funny kid, and he and I began to play at talking like hillbillies, since that was a theme on Ozarks' billboards and signs. We stopped at a grocery store, and I was going to go in and get a few things while Kathy waited with the children. Kathy reminded me that we needed some paper cups. When Robert heard that, he said, "We need some cuuups, Paaaaaa," imitating the dialect that Tom and I had been trying out.

Rob was four, and he had picked up the sound. Maybe lots of kids could do that. I'm not sure. But I doubted it. I suspected right then that Rob was going to be something special. Now he's raising a boy who is so much the same. And what a great father Rob is. I was at the hospital the day little Billy was born. Kathy and I were waiting just outside the delivery room. As soon as Billy, named after Kathy's father William Hurst, was born—and Stacy, Rob's wife, had had a chance to see him—a nurse brought him to our side of the room. We had stepped inside by then, with Stacy's mom and sister. As the nurse washed little Billy, Rob looked down at him and said, "My son." Then he began to sob.

I did too, and so did both the grandmas and Billy's young aunt. My mind went back to "my son." My baby. Those baths and those smiles.

It's nice to watch Rob with Billy. He's not afraid to change a diaper, and he's very involved in raising and nurturing his boy. My own dad didn't know how to do that, and I never felt much emotional attachment to him, but my sons are close to their kids, and so is my son-in-law. I would like to think that some of the change in tradition in our family began that summer of 1973.

Some of my favorite memories are connected to "big brother" Tom. He was born in Seattle when I was in graduate school there, and in our student ward he was called "Terrible Tommy." He was one of the busiest, most intense kids who ever lived. As a toddler, he had gone about tearing down anything in his path, moving almost faster than Kathy could run. At five, in that summer of '73, he was not so likely to pull all the pans out of the cupboard or pour laundry soap over his head, but he was always going, going, going. He would want me to play with him on the floor, and I would hardly get down before he was off and running, with something new in mind. He drove the older girls crazy, and he was not easy on his sister, whom he would tease and harass.

The low moment of my parenting life might have been the day I caught Tommy choking his sister. I lost control. I grabbed him around the neck (only lightly, I'd like to think) as I shouted, "So do you like that? Do you like someone to choke you?" Later, in a calmer moment, I realized I had tried to teach a child not to be violent by using violence. The logic didn't hold up.

Still, from the time Tommy was very little, he would always sit still for a book. In spite of his wildness, he would calm down when I would put him on my lap and read to him. Some of the best moments of my summer came at times when I got Tommy, and usually Amy with him, on my lap, and we read together. That was something that continued as the kids grew up.

Once, when Tommy was maybe six, he wanted to hear a story and I was teaching *Beowulf* at the time, so I read him a modern-language prose translation. We read the tale every night for two or three weeks, and boy, did he like that story. Any guy who could fight a monster, and do it underwater, was a hero to Tommy. But in the end, Beowulf died, and I looked up from the book to see that my little son was crying. I taught the tale in many a sophomore-level lit course, but Tommy was my only student who ever cried for *Beowulf*.

When Tommy was nine, Amy seven, and Rob four, I read all of *David Copperfield* to them. It took us all winter, reading almost every night. Rob was awfully young, but he wanted to be in on the reading. I remember finishing passages and then asking Rob if he had understood. If he hadn't gotten all of it, Tommy took great pride, with Amy's help, in explaining the whole thing to little brother. The next winter we read *Great Expectations*. (Victorian lit, especially Dickens, was my specialty.)

The fact is, I started reading to Tommy almost out of self-defense. It was one way to calm him down. But Tommy grew into Tom, who majored in English in college, as I had done. All three of our kids love books to this day, and when our family gets together we are soon talking about what we've been reading. Never once in their lives has one of them experienced a Christmas without receiving a book from Kathy and me, and I'm the one who gets the yearly assignment of choosing the books.

So I think of that summer, and one nice memory is Tommy on my lap, his head against my shoulder. I had a favorite trick of reading something wrong on purpose, and that would make him laugh because he knew all our books by heart. He loved to correct me and tell me the right word. He had a wonderful laugh and a quick response. Sometimes he would "read" the books to me, since he knew them as well as I did. And the child we sometimes suspected of hyperactivity would sit with me for as long as I could find the time to read to him. What I'm glad of is that we did read together in spite of the craziness I was seeing around me. I don't know whether we did as much of that as we could have. But we did read. And I'm glad Tom loves books. It makes me think I might have done one thing right.

Tom's major in college, as I said, was English, but the great love he developed was for theater and for acting. After his undergraduate years, he ended up studying at the American Repertory Theatre at Harvard, and then he went to New York City to try to "make it" as an actor. By then he had married Kristen, an actress herself, and the two put in some challenging years as Tom pursued his dream. Tom and Kris got their own baby boy while living in New York, and the two juggled dreams with practicalities. Tom ended up being a mom himself—actually for a much longer time than I did—and he experienced a lot of the same frustrations. He had it in his head that he would be a great caregiver himself, but he ended up feeling that he hadn't lived up to his own expectations. Still, I watch him with his kids and I can tell he has a great relationship with Steven, whom he cared for in New York, and also with Carrie and Tal, who came later.

But here's the thing. He wanted to be an actor, dreamed of it, and at the same time began to see what it was costing his family. And so he gave it up. He went back to grad school and then went to work as a business consultant. He travels all over the world now, and that's tough on his wife, so he hopes he won't always be gone so much, but what impressed me was that his family came first to him. That idea surely came from all sorts of sources, but I'd like to think that summer of 1973 had something to do with his acquiring that value.

And then there's Amy, now a mother of four. She's on the other end of this whole process I've been talking about. Stubborn little Amy—the child who would get something in her head and absolutely not give it up. She has three little boys who have some of that in them too, but she's got a three-year-old daughter, Katie, exactly the age Amy was that summer, who is now giving her fits.

Katie gets something in her head, and forget it, she's going to fight to the death. The little girl is raising unreasonableness to an art form. Okay, so I do laugh a little at that, but it's only because I know the day will come when stubbornness will turn into tenacity and Katie will be as magnificent as her mother, who believes in things, cares about things, and stands up for what she cares about. Amy lives in a whirlwind, with four young kids, and she gets as stressed out as I did that summer, but she persists in doing good wherever she can—in her family, ward, and community. She takes on much more than she should but manages to get an immense amount done. She's a better mom than I was, but she often doesn't think so. She's plagued with the same feelings of guilt.

I remember Amy, at three, with her blonde hair in pigtails, a lot like her own little light-haired Katie. And I remember her wrapping her arms around her daddy's neck, squeezing me, and making me feel like a wonderful dad—even though I was only a barely adequate summer replacement. She would decide that she wanted to put on a striped shirt with plaid shorts, and I would tell her that didn't look good. Of course, my opinion meant nothing. She knew what looked good, and that was that. We have some pictures of her we cherish now, her in her odd choices for clothes, looking just as lovely as she thought she did. (I've noticed, too, that when she decorates her house, she puts patterns of fabrics and colors together I wouldn't expect. And they work. So what do I know?)

I got very frustrated with Amy at times, and scolded her, but she would forget quickly and adorn me with kisses. She was always so loving, and she still is. Later, when Amy was a teenager, she was intense in that way that adolescent girls tend to be. By then I was writing full-time, so when she came home from school I was there. She would come downstairs to my office (we lived in Provo, Utah, by then), and she would say, "How was your day, Dad?" I would tell her that it was uneventful, or about like most days for a writer (spent in front of a computer), and then she would pronounce her day as *wonderful* or *horrible*. Those seemed to be the only two choices. Some friend had said something about her, or she hadn't been asked out to a dance yet, or the opposite: she *had* been asked and she was excited, but she needed to decide what she was going to wear. Whatever the issue, it was always *very* important, and so she and I would often go for a drive, buy us a soft drink, and talk things over. The boys played sports by then, and usually weren't home that time of day, so Amy and I often spent some of that time together.

We still do. Rarely does a day go by without her calling me. I lean away from my computer for a minute, and we talk. (I'll admit, I'm sometimes in my own little writer's world and don't give her my full attention any better than I did when she was three, but I love to talk to her.) She's still pretty intense about everything, too. I'm going on a trip soon, and Kathy can't go, so Brad, Amy's husband, is going to take a week off work (Big deal, a mom for a *week!*), and Amy and I are going to Thailand. There are two things I know for sure: we'll have a great time and we'll talk and talk and talk. Maybe we would have become as close anyway, but at least in my imagination, that summer of 1973 actually did bond me to Amy and to the boys just as I hoped it would. It simply didn't happen quite in the way I expected.

All My "Daughters"

———— ❈ ————

It's an interesting thing to watch your children grow up—and turn out almost better than you dared to hope. And then the cycle starts over and you watch them go through some of the same experiences with their own kids. Amy has four children nine and under; Kristen has three seven and under; and Stacy has her first and another on the way. When the whole family gets together, chaos returns, and I think of the days when our kids were little. Among the grandchildren we have three older boys who have been as intense and active as Tom ever was (but they're starting to grow out of that a little now—or at least they'll sit in front of our PlayStation for hours at a time). We have our two girls, four and three, who are geniuses at getting into trouble and frankly noisier than the boys. Next, we have two-year-old Billy, who is busy himself and tries to keep up with the older kids. Plus, now we have two baby boys, crawling, and about to walk. In the midst of the bedlam, when the whole family was together recently, I asked the three moms to tell me about their lives. They laughed a lot, and so did I, but some of the stuff they're going through is only funny after some time passes. The truth is, life is not easy for any one of them.

Amy talked about Sundays. Hers is a common story. Her husband serves in a bishopric, so he leaves home early, and she has four kids to get ready for church. And then, at church, Brad sits on the stand, so Amy has to "keep it together" in a pew somewhere. Sunday is her most exhausting day and she wonders when her "day of rest" is ever going to come.

The problem starts, of course, with getting everyone up, fed, scrubbed, and dressed nicely for church. Michael and David, at nine and seven, can dress themselves, but they don't always get around to it. So Amy reminds them, her voice rising as the minutes tick away, while she does Katie's hair. Katie loves to dress up in pretty things, and she likes her hair to be nice; she simply doesn't like the process of getting it that way. (She knows how to shriek, too.) And little Samuel wants to be fed and changed and played with, Sunday or not. So if he puts up a howl while all the other stuff is going on, Amy has to do what she can to calm him and then get back to the pretty hair and the boys who dawdle.

When it's finally time, Amy realizes that the boys' hair never actually got combed or they couldn't find their church pants and are only now getting finished, someone's shoes are always lost or a belt or a hair ribbon is missing. David has to be convinced to put his Game Boy away, and Michael has to be reminded to take his scriptures. Katie is still mad from the hair ordeal and announces that she's not getting in the car. "I don't *want* to go to church," she's saying, and by then, Amy is losing just enough of her mind to say something like, "Well, neither do I, little girl, but we're going anyway."

So finally she gets them all into the SUV and they drive the three blocks or so to church, usually a few minutes late. Since her sacrament meeting is scheduled last, she deposits the older kids in Primary and hurries off to Sunday School, which she likes but doesn't always get to sit through—depending on what kind of mood Sam is in. After wrestling with Sam another hour during Relief Society, she gathers her chickens together again and heads to sacrament meeting. By then everyone is tired. Amy searches desperately for a bench in the back but some weeks she's too late, and she has to march the whole gang up front. It's only then that she realizes that David has his Game Boy with him, and he's walking down the aisle, punching the buttons. Brad is sitting on the stand, looking embarrassed, but he knows: he'd better not say anything. He can see in Amy's red face that she's only inches from turning into Mount St. Helens. The kids finally pile into a pew, and Amy begins to whisper warnings. She wonders, all the same, how long before TROUBLE will begin.

The kids usually last until the sacrament is passed, but not always. Most often, it's the baby who first puts up a fuss, and the question is, what to do? Should she take Sam out and tell the rest to stay? What will they do while she's gone? What if one of the boys gets in a fight with his sister and hurts her in front of the whole ward? But the alternative is to lead the whole bunch back out, the same way she brought them in. For some reason, the boys' shirttails are hanging out *again,* and Katie's hair is coming loose. The kids have crayons and coloring books and quiet books strewn across the bench. Should Amy carry all that out or should she leave the mess and hope she can get back to it someday? The bishop has asked the members not to bring Cheerios anymore, and she doesn't, but right now she wishes she had something to offer for a bribe.

So she chooses to threaten the three older kids with bodily injury if they act up—lovingly, of course, in a soft voice—and then she quietly slips out to the foyer, carrying Sam, who is crying hard by then. But she's not out there two minutes before Katie comes wandering out, and then in another minute, David. Finally, Michael walks out and says he didn't want to sit by himself. So instead of creating a parade, and one big disturbance, she's managed to create four. Sam has quieted down, but dare she take the chance and form another parade as they all walk back?

More often than not, she chooses to stay in the foyer, then returns to pick up all her stuff before she heads home. For a long time she was in her Primary presidency, and managing all that with a baby in her arms was always complicated. Brad tried to help when he could, but there were lots of demands on him, too. (Amy served with other young women who also had babies, and the three did lots of trading off and helping each other.)

Amy has lots of Sunday stories. One week Katie decided she was going to walk to the stand and sit by her daddy. What Brad saw as she approached was that Katie was wearing her "Dora the Explorer" shoes. Brad was sitting next to a high councilor and a member of the stake presidency, so he picked her up quickly. He hoped the brethren wouldn't notice the shoes. But when he whispered to Katie that she shouldn't wear those shoes to church from now on, Katie said, in a loud voice, "Mom said it was okay. She said, '*Fine!* Wear your Dora shoes!'" Brad glanced sideways and smiled a little. The two brothers smiled back. They have kids, too—and wives.

Kristen sat through a long sermon once, trying to keep her kids from crawling under the seats or fighting over crayons. At the end of the talk, the speaker said, "Amen," and a little girl nearby, in a loud voice, said, "Fin-a-*leeee*." Hey, it wasn't one of her kids—for once.

The three-hour block actually does come to an end, although a physicist I know believes that the LDS three-hour meeting period has actually caused some sort of bend in space, and what appears to be three hours on a clock is actually closer to sixteen hours. I'm sure a lot of young moms would accept that theory on faith—or without any.

By the time Amy gets home and all the kids start asking for dinner, she's not sure she wants to put a nice pot roast in the oven and wait—while the kids get more upset. What she really wants is to lock herself in her room and take a nap for an hour, but Brad is still at church, counting the tithing money and doing a couple of youth interviews. Monday starts to look pretty good. At least the older kids will be in school.

It's funny, though, how Amy responded when I asked her what she got out of church if it was so difficult. She admitted that she has wondered at times, but then she said, "It's not an option, not to go. I want my kids to know that's what we do." She talked, too, about the support she gets from other mothers—sometimes out in the foyer together. She teaches in Relief Society now, and she says she loves that time with her sisters (and her mom didn't make her say that), even though Sam can be restless. She told me, "There's always something I hear in Sunday School or Relief Society, or even sacrament meeting—which is the hardest—something I can use that week." She talked, too, of *taking* the sacrament, which is one of the things that gets her through her difficult times. She described watching her son Michael being baptized or her kids getting up to give their talks or to say their parts in Primary programs. She even talked about weeks when one of her kids has been sick, and she's had to miss church. "No matter how hard it is to go, I still miss being there."

So my little baby girl is a grownup now, doing what Kathy had to do when I was in the bishopric. That famous summer of 1973, I only had the kids all week. Sundays, I merely had to be at the church most of the day. That was my day of rest. Real moms are not so lucky.

Amy, Kristen, and Stacy also talked about the way children make a minor chore into a massive one. Let's say, for instance, that just as one of them is preparing dinner, she realizes that she doesn't have any cumin, or whatever, and her recipe calls for that very whatever she doesn't have. Well, there's a store not far away. No problem. But the oldest of these moms' kids are not old enough to look after the younger ones for a few minutes, and that means everyone has to go.

In Amy's case, that means getting four kids out of the house—finding the shoes, getting them on, strapping the baby into his car seat, and then getting all four buckled up. The boys can do their own seat belts, and Michael can help Katie, and sometimes it works that way—but more often than not, the kids aren't too happy about this little trip, since they just got pulled away from a favorite TV show or video game, and sometimes, little ones get cross with each other, and sometimes a mother tells them to stop it or she'll destroy every electronic device they own. Along with all that, sometimes buckles don't want to work, and sometimes the baby starts to cry.

All these moms described the same ordeal, even Stacy, with only one child (but a two-year-old, and remember, Stacy is dealing with morning sickness). Just getting children into a car is a major task, and when the mom gets to the store, she has to get everyone out of all those buckles again. Then she hurries into the store, watching all the kids and keeping an eye on the parking-lot traffic. She finally makes it inside and now she has to get the baby into a cart and decide how many more of the kids she wants to pile into the thing. By now, the older ones are taking off to look at something they want, and Mom is saying, "No, not today. I just need a couple of things and then we're leaving."

About then Mom takes a good look at the kids and realizes they look like those trashy children she used to see in stores—the ones that made her wonder what kind of mothers were raising them. Stuff is smeared on their clothes and faces. Their hair is disheveled.

Shoes are untied. Wait! One of them has *no* shoes. When Mom asks him about that, he says, "You didn't *tell* me to put my shoes on."

These are moments that kids have a feel for. They have great instincts and they know that Mom is never so vulnerable as when she's in public, or when she's in a hurry and doesn't want a fuss. So they attack. "Can we have . . ." the sentence always starts, and the answer is a very firm, "No. It's time for dinner. You don't need any junk."

Each child has a technique. At three, a tantrum is a wonderful method. At seven, a better approach is begging incessantly while whining and accusing one's mother of never buying any of this or that. At nine, it's negotiation: "If you'll get us this or that, we won't eat it until after dinner." (Michael is a bright and good boy, but he understands the Eddy Haskell approach to adults: "Gee, Mother, wouldn't Dad like a nice treat for dessert tonight? He works so hard, and he just loves chocolate-chip cookies. You're a great mom, but you really don't bake cookies very often.")

Kids sense the nerve-wracking and embarrassing power of a tantrum; the wearing-down process of incessant begging; the guilt in the argument "You don't bake . . ." And babies seem to sense that this can be their moment, too—an excellent time to cry. Many a mom has bought Ding Dongs after vowing not to; Gummi Worms, which she hates; or sugar-coated, chocolate-filled cereal, which she believes was created by Satan.

Kristen was in a store with Carrie one day when the little sweetheart put up a tremendous fuss about something she wanted. When Kris told her she couldn't have it, Carrie began to scream, "You're not my mommy. You're not my mommy." People kept looking at Kris as though she might have kidnapped innocent little Carrie with the lovely dimple and the soft blue eyes. I think the story ends with Kris giving in, as I recall. This is the same Carrie who once screamed for an hour and a half without once stopping because Kris wouldn't give her a lollipop for breakfast. This is something else kids understand. In a store, five minutes of screaming might work, but at home, the process takes a lot longer. (To Kristen's credit, Carrie did finally lose the lollipop-for-breakfast battle.) But Carrie is as persistent—to use a nice word—as any child I know (except for her cousin Katie. Oh, yeah, and that mom of Katie's we talked about earlier.)

So anyway, the cumin or the Cocoa Puffs or the powdered-sugar donuts or the Match Box racecar—and whatever else—get purchased, and then Mom heads back to the car and the buckling starts over. By the time she gets home, an hour has passed. By then Dad has come home and is wondering what the strange mix is, sitting in a bowl on the kitchen counter—without cumin. There's something, perhaps, to be said for the days of little corner markets and huge cars with no seat belts, with little kids bouncing dangerously from front seat to back and then up front again. In the name of safety, the mind has become an easy thing to waste.

By the way, all three of these mothers agreed that it didn't help much to take husbands along to the store. "They're like one more kid you have to look after. They wander off, don't help with the kids, and want to buy as much junk food as the kids do." (I don't know about this *younger generation;* I wasn't like that.)

All my "daughters" talked about times when they capitulate under pressure. They laughed nervously, ashamed of themselves, but aware that at least they are finding ways to survive. Stacy told about the morning that she was wiped-out tired and Billy was up with the first sign of summer light. She gave him a big piece of cake and put him in front of *Bob the Builder* while she slept for another half hour. "Hey, cake has wheat and milk and eggs and stuff," she told me. "That's breakfast food." Another time she was so tired of Billy pulling all the toilet paper off the roll in the bathroom that she put him in the bathtub (with no water) and gave him a roll of his own. That kept him busy long enough for her to take care of a few things she needed to do.

Kristen once let Steven watch *The Lion King* over and over all day. "I know that's really bad to do," she said, "but *killing* a child is a lot worse." But then, Kristen has an extra level of challenge. Tom's work takes him away from home about half the time, and his consulting trips often come in bunches, meaning that he is hardly home at all for several weeks at a time. Kris talked to me about the struggle she has when there's no one there to help her with *any-thing*. No one comes home at night to play with the kids. "Steven and Carrie like to get down on the floor and wrestle, or get thrown in the air. They like someone to give them 'noogies' or throw a ball with them. But it's just not my kind of thing. They just miss all that when Tom is gone." What's worse, Tom often gets home jet-lagged from flying across an ocean, and it's not easy for him to respond immediately to Kristen's or the kids' needs. Many times, he's home for a weekend or just a few days, knows he has to get lawns mowed and jobs done around the house, wants to get his home teaching in, and is on conference calls with clients and co-workers for hours. The kids want him, and Kristen needs desperately to have a break, and she needs time to talk to him. If that doesn't happen, she feels cheated when he takes off again. When Kristen has to do *everything,* from taking out the garbage to refereeing kids in a dispute—with no letup, around the clock—she wears down, and she feels terribly lonely. "If I see one of my friends, I practically talk her head off," she told me. "Tom calls home, but it's hard for him, too, if I spend the whole time he's on the phone telling him how hard my life is."

So what about single moms? Right now they're asking themselves, "That's my life, and no one ever comes home to play with the kids, mow the lawn—or talk to me." And they're right. I can't imagine how hard that would be.

The young mothers also talked about how easily they sometimes give in to bribery techniques. If Amy has to run a few errands, the kids start begging for her to stop for treats at a convenience store. "Okay, okay. If you'll let me stop at the bank and go to the post office, we'll stop and buy you all . . ." Let me remind you that Michael is a fine young man, starting to grow up now, but he's still a little fixated on those treats. One day Amy got the kids into the car for a trip to the grocery store and Michael must have been thinking a lot about the goodies he hoped to bargain for. When Amy ran back to the house for something, she tripped and fell on the driveway and broke her little finger. She was sitting on the ground crying when Michael got worried about her. He got himself unbuckled and came to her aid. Amy, with strain in her voice, explained that she thought she had broken her finger and she might have to go to the hospital. Michael apparently saw the trip to the store vanishing. He asked her, "After you go to the hospital, on the way back, do you think you could stop for some snacks?" Amy admitted to me that her response was quite unmotherly and made Michael feel terrible, and she still feels guilty about what she said. (I think I won't quote this one.)

But then, either way Mom handles the situation, she feels guilty. If she says no, she hates to disappoint her kids; if she says yes, she fears she's making them fat—and we hear every day that mothers are letting their kids eat too much junk.

All three mothers said they worry about what they're doing to their kids: "I see how they mimic me, and it's scary." Billy, at two, likes to take credit cards from Stacy's wallet, and he knows what to do with them. He pretends to swipe them, with just the right motion.

One day Brad called home from work to see how things were going. Katie picked up the phone. "Mommy's mad," she said. "You need to come home right now and fix that *darn* computer." Of course, Amy had no idea where Katie had picked up that word—and actually, the word wasn't *darn*.

These young mothers live in a strange world, they tell me. They get so far behind on current events, they feel utterly uninformed, and yet they know the names of all the characters on *Arthur*. They try to watch a little *Oprah* when they can, but they're convinced that daytime television is actually a plot to make women stupid. When their husbands come home, they quiz them to learn anything that sounds like the sort of information grown-ups talk about.

Wait a minute. This is starting to sound familiar. I've been there, as I recall. But these younger men aren't like me. The three moms told me that their husbands watch the kids sometimes, but when the women get back, their men have only played with the kids, or they've gone about whatever it was they needed to do themselves. The house is a disaster, the kids haven't been fed, and then the guys say, quite innocently, "I don't know what's so tough about watching kids. We had fun while you were gone."

So what's good about being a mother? I asked them that, too. Kristen pointed at my two little granddaughters. Our family gets together to celebrate all the birthdays that happen in a month, and on this day Carrie was one of the birthday kids. Billie, with help from his dad, had chosen a present for Carrie: a pink feather boa, a "diamond" tiara with matching earrings, and pinkish lip gloss. (I did mention, didn't I, that Carrie's parents were performers?) The two girls were sitting at the kitchen table putting "makeup" on each other. A few minutes before, they had attacked me, claimed I was chocolate, and tried to eat me. Num, num, num, num. Carrie had been swishing all around the house with her boa around her neck, scattering pink feathers behind her (while I was taking pictures).

Kristen, of course, was exactly right. These little girls can be hard on the nerves, but they are absolutely brimming with emotion, fun, and exhilaration. Even in the midst of the madness, Kristen said, she can't help laughing at intense little Carrie, who is so intelligent, so dimpled, so excited about whatever she is doing. We decided that Carrie and Katie are going to be amazing women, full of commitment, independence, vitality, and yes, stubbornness. As a matter of fact, they'll be like their mothers, and, of course, I don't want to brag, but I had something to do with raising one of those women—who has turned out *just fine.*

Stacy says that sometimes she'll be standing in her bathroom in her old purple robe, drying her hair with a blow dryer. Her hair will be frizzed out in all directions, but Billy will say, "You're pretty, Mommy." He likes the look. He likes his mommy. And she can't resist his little gap-toothed smile any more than I could resist his daddy's.

I watched little Sam with his mom. He likes to kiss her. He washes her whole face with his "wet ones," and it really is as though she's chocolate and he's num-num-numming her. I was holding him that same Sunday evening, and he just kept looking to his mom as though she were the only human in the world who really mattered to him.

Amy also told us a wonderful story. I've mentioned David. He's seven now, and we think he's over his grumpy period, which lasted about four years (no exaggeration). Dear David has sometimes been a trial for Amy. He was the kid who refused to cooperate. If we wanted a family picture, he would decide, for no reason we knew, that he didn't want to be in it. He fought Amy on almost everything for such a long time. On top of that, he was always the one to get his feelings hurt. He needed a good chewing out rather often, but he would either react with anger or he would be crushed. Maybe he was a middle kid who was feeling the pinch. We didn't know, but Amy worried about him for a long time.

But lately, he's been coming out of all that. He'll give me a hug when I see him, and he'll talk to me about things going on in his life. He's nuts about his Nana, too. ("Can't you stay and play a little longer?" he asks her when we leave.) One day, recently, he told Amy that he had invited a friend to come to their house and play. He said that the friend was "a little different," but that didn't matter. Amy called the boy's mother to make the invitation official, and it was then that the mother explained that the boy was a Down's Syndrome child and he had never in his life been invited to a friend's house. Amy assured the woman that she welcomed him.

When mother and son arrived, Amy could see that the mom was nervous. She stayed for a time, trying to make sure that her son was going to be okay. David listened to the talk and seemed to pick up on the mother's worries. He walked over and took the mentally challenged boy by the hand, and then he looked back at the mother. "It's okay," he reassured her. "We'll just go in the bedroom and play. We'll have fun." The boys went off to the bedroom. When Amy looked at the boy's mother, she was crying. So was Amy.

I'm not really surprised by any of this. No one is more compassionate than my Amy. If her children mimic her worst moments, why shouldn't they mimic her at her best? However "active" my grandchildren are—and however wearing on their mothers—they are picking up the values of their parents, and they have good parents. The kids, I believe, sense what their parents are made of, and they're acquiring their own good hearts. I have the feeling another generation is going to come out all right. They're going to have their problems and weaknesses, and they're going to make mistakes. Some of them will have their Papa's impatience, perhaps, or his seemingly natural tendency toward skepticism, but if we all love them enough and *show* them what we believe, a good share of our best traits will transfer.

Honest, moms, you're doing all right. I learned that summer, it's always good to take a peek at your children when they're asleep at night. They really are angels even if they've acted like little devils all day.

Teen Angels?

—— ⁎ ——

Oh, yeah. There's something we're forgetting. Children turn into teenagers. Mothers think the hard times are over when the kids trot off to school, but then comes that "delivery-boy" era when all life seems scheduled around soccer practice and piano lessons. Mom begins looking forward to the day when the kids can drive themselves. But then come those Saturday nights and the worries about "where are they and what are they doing?"

You know you're the parent of a teenager when you become an embarrassment to your child, instead of the other way around. Once, at a BYU football game, on a very cold day, everyone stood and cheered for a Cougar touchdown. After the cheer, when everyone was still standing, I started hopping up and down just a little, trying to get my body warm. Amy, who was in junior high at the time, looked at me and said, "Dad, what are you doing?"

"Getting warm," I said.

"But no one else is doing that."

Dear compassionate Amy, so full of understanding of others, with a master's degree in social work. *Now.* But at thirteen, even though she liked to talk to me *alone,* she preferred that I stay out of sight when her friends were around. My kids all told me they were embarrassed that I wrote children's books because, after all, what if a friend read one of them and thought it was *lame?*

But Tom was our most trying adolescent. The boy couldn't tell time. If we told him to come home by eleven, he came in at eleven fifteen—to see what we would do, I think. And if we didn't do enough, he would come in at eleven-thirty, just to see how far he could push us. It's not like he ever got into serious trouble. (Rob flirted more with danger, but he knew enough to come home on time, so he got away with more.) Tom was the kid everyone wants: good student, school leader, athletic, and all the rest. But he didn't believe in sleep, never had, so why should he come home at eleven and then have nothing to do? He was our first, and his friends were mostly younger siblings. So with him I was especially uptight, but he knew his job: to break down the barriers for his sister and brother.

In some ways those years from about twelve to seventeen are the dark ages. Kids who have been so lovely and willing to kiss and hug their parents go around as though they are hiding some evil secret behind their suspicious eyes. They do all that glandular stuff and look pretty awful in the process. They suddenly have these wild emotions that spring them from ecstatic to depressed in a matter of minutes. It's the era when they like anything you don't like: music, movies, slang, whatever. Or they do whatever you wouldn't want them to do. I got a call from the BYU police department one day. Some boys, *in my car,* had been observed stealing a bowling ball from the Wilkinson Center. I questioned Rob when he got home and he fessed up. But at least he and his friends had a good reason for heisting the bowling ball: they wanted to roll it off the side of a mountain. Rob hunted down the ball, out in the snow, and took it back to BYU, and they didn't send him to jail. Did I mention he's an attorney now?

I got through all that, but it was their view of me that was as hard as anything to accept. I've always suspected that I had a fair degree of coolness. I mean, I was "one of the guys" in high school. But suddenly, when my kids hit their teens, I was so "out of it," and so was Kathy. *"Stubid"* all over again. We didn't know what was going on anymore; we didn't know what was cool to wear; we would say things like, "I can't even understand the lyrics those guys are singing."

But there were some upsides to those years, too. First of all, teenagers are fun. I laughed *at* my kids at times (with my hand over my mouth), but I also laughed with them a lot. And their friends were always just as excitable and zany, and Kathy and I loved to have them all in our home. Tom once announced that he had some friends coming over. He bought a bag of M&Ms and a sack of potato chips—and then *dozens,* maybe a hundred kids showed up. Teenagers were in the house, outside, all over the neighborhood. And I was out of town. But Kathy got through it, and she was always a great favorite with our kids' friends.

There's another upside. Inside that pimply exterior is an eighteen-year-old about to emerge. At about eighteen, they return. They become humans, and it's all worth it. Three of the most painful days of our lives, for Kathy and me, were the days our eighteen-year-olds left for college. I think of Rob, as we backed from our driveway on the way to the airport. I looked over, and tears were running down his face. Or Tom, when we visited him at Thanksgiving time, his first fall away, and his tears dropping onto a restaurant table. I think of Amy, as we dropped her off at her dorm, holding onto us even though we weren't going to be all that far away. It's then a parent thinks, *These teenagers are not so bad after all.*

I know that things don't always work out well. I know that some young people really do mess up. Some even turn against all the things we've tried to teach them. But I think the best, most fundamental traits we possess do resonate with young people. They know who we are, and if our hearts are right, theirs will usually not get too far off course. Those who stray often come back. And those who don't have not finished their eternal growth. What we do is what we can, and we should never give up on our children, never stop loving them.

A Real Mother

—◦ ❋ ◦—

A lot of what I know about mothers, I actually learned from my wife. Except for that summer of '73, she was the one at home with our kids when they were little. I did get my eyes opened during that time, and after that, I had a greater appreciation for the things she was doing. I watch her now and still marvel at what she does.

Kathy is, in principle, an organized person. Or at least she would like to be. She loves order, and she's always making headlong attempts to get her world shaped up. The trouble is, the world resists—especially kids. She also takes on far too much. She likes to read, likes to sew, likes to quilt, likes to study the gospel, likes to exercise, likes to travel . . . and the list goes on and on. She can never manage everything, so she makes hard stabs at getting enough regimen in her life to do as much as possible. One of her ways of doing that is to do about four hundred things a day, with a plan to spend fifteen minutes at each. The trouble is, that adds up to a hundred hours.

One of her devices to help create order in our home, learned from Relief Society perhaps, was the "Friday box." If a kid left a toy on the floor or dropped a shoe in the living room, it went into the box, and the kids didn't get it back until Friday. She loves a system like that because it teaches the children responsibility and it is all mapped out with specific guidelines. I'll even agree, it was a very good system, one other mothers might want to learn from her. But it would always lose momentum after a while, like so many of her attempts to organize us.

Okay. I'm going to admit something here. The kids had a way of undermining her plans, but her biggest problem was often her husband. At some deep level I'm an anarchist. I've never tried to act like a boss to Kathy. (It wouldn't work anyway; our kids didn't get their independence from the tooth fairy.) On the other hand, I don't like to be bossed, either. I hasten to add, it was not that Kathy was trying to boss me, but she was always trying to convince me to set up a rule I would have to live by.

I knew better than to fight the system, so I would buy in, convince the kids I was on Mom's side, not theirs, and actually try to prove it. But I could always see the flaws. What if one of the kids left a shoe in the living room, couldn't get it back, but needed it to wear to school? Kathy would usually want to add another rule: "You have to wear your church shoes to school," "You have to give up a toy to get the shoe back," or something of that sort, and that sounds reasonable, but we kids—or I mean, *the* kids—still didn't like it.

Let's be even a little more honest about all this. Aren't all men really boys? I'm not sure that all women grow up, but most of them seem to. Maybe an occasional man does too, but most of us know, deep down, that we're kids and we're living with a grownup. We admire all that responsibility women demonstrate, but I think we resent it, too. Part of the way we fight back is to go to the other extreme. If women use lace cloths and flowers on their tables at Relief Society, we go out of our way to be a bunch of easygoing good guys in our meetings. (Of course, this sometimes extends all the way to being ill-prepared, and I'm not going to joke about that. It's a problem.) But you see my point. A husband is often the enemy of a well-organized home, and one of his sneaky techniques (to which I will admit a degree of culpability) is to align themselves with their kids. I've been known to jump on board, support Kathy's latest plan, and then watch it fail with a tiny bit of guilty satisfaction.

Kathy liked to use a "chore wheel." It had a spinner on it, and each week at family home evening we would spin the wheel and receive our work assignments. But kids have a thing about any perceived unfairness: "I had to do that last week" or "Why do I always get the hard jobs?" Clearly, though, the best way to resist a plan like that is merely to let its momentum die out slowly. It's as though gravity itself doesn't like an organized family and finally pulls it down. The kids would slack off, and I would take a stand with Kathy that that just wouldn't do, but each renewal would take more effort, and finally Kathy would know that she was swimming upstream and her own mate was taking the easy way, drifting out toward the depths of the ocean along with her offspring.

Mind you, it was not that I resisted the chores. I am sort of half grownup, and I'm not lazy. But as you've heard, it always seems easier to me to do a job than to get the kids to do it.

Kathy, however, would never give up. She would spring back up as one of her programs began to dwindle and fail, and she would get it all going again. The Friday box made many returns, and so did the chore wheel. We also had a box that we drew from to determine what we would do for family home evening and who would teach the lesson. I now know that the kids got onto that system and while Kathy wasn't watching they would find a preferred slip of paper—"roller skating" or "ice cream"—and put it on top of all the slips that said "lesson." I didn't help them on that one; I learned only recently that those little scamps did such a thing. (But on the other hand, I do like to go roller skating; why should I notice that the slip kept reappearing?)

I'm repentant now. Kathy was always trying to get us up early to read the scriptures, and I had nothing at all against the scripture part; it was the early I didn't like. And the kids didn't like it either. But she got us up enough that we did put in more time with the scriptures than we would have otherwise. We would often fall into the paths of weakness, and I didn't do enough to help her keep the practice going, I admit, but at least I do feel bad about some of those things. I even like the idea of the chore chart, now that I look back on it, and just let me say right here that I recommend it to my children. Be like your mom; be grownups—even you men. (See, I do support her.)

Here's the main thing—all kidding aside—that Kathy gave our

kids. They knew how much she cared about them, and they knew how far she would go to support them. She wanted them to learn to work, and she was right about that, and she wanted them to know the scriptures—right again—and she believed a certain strictness (a strictness I had never learned and couldn't fake) would give them structure. She always worked hard to be a good mother. Our kids differ, and they have their weaknesses, but I must admit, honestly, that more of their good traits come from Kathy than from me.

For most of us, our best qualities can also be our worst. Kathy would be the first to say that she regrets, now, that she sometimes pushed too hard. But if she expected a lot of our kids, she also expected plenty of herself as well. And she knew there were times to break her own rules. Amy reminded me of a time when she was looking for something to wear to Senior Prom. She and Kathy went shopping together and found a beautiful Jessica McClintock dress, back when those were the big thing. Amy tried the dress on and fell in love with it. But she looked at the price, and it was just too much. Kathy loved the dress, too, and she understood there were times when her budget, no matter how much she longed to be strict about it, needed to be adjusted. She bought the dress, and more than the dress, mom and daughter shared the moment. Amy has never forgotten what her mother's adaptability meant to her that day.

You have to understand, I would have bought the dress without a second thought. And maybe that makes me a good guy. But budgeting was much more important to Kathy, and thank goodness it was, because I'm a terrible impulse buyer. What meant so much to Amy was that she knew her mom didn't think we could afford the dress, but she also knew this was a time for an exception. I fear that sounds materialistic, and maybe it is, to care so much for a mere article of clothing, but the dream of a senior to look her best at her prom might be wrong to call mere materialism. Kathy understood that it was something more than that for Amy right then.

There's another Amy/Kathy story that's a classic. Amy was listening to the radio one day when she was in high school. She called the station in response to a contest and won a record album. Yes, it was an actual "record" back then, vinyl and everything. So Kathy drove her down to the station to pick up the prize. Amy was bumping off the walls with excitement, but when she came outside with the album, Kathy took a look and gulped. She wasn't at all sure it was music Amy ought to be listening to (nor was she certain it was bad). She described her concerns to Amy and told her that she might want to reconsider accepting the prize. Amy, in her anger, told her mother there was nothing wrong with the singer (even though she wasn't so sure herself, she now admits). Kathy finally said she wanted to talk to me about it—but it was another time when I was out of town.

Amy was too mad to let things ride. (Did I mention that Amy can be stubborn?) She put on a real show. She went to her room, put the record on her portable player, and cranked up the sound as high as it would go. Then, after listening for a while, and getting no reaction, she took the fight to another level. She walked out of her room, faced Kathy, and told her, as best as Amy now remembers, "I don't know what it will ever take to get your trust. I get good grades; I go to church; I do everything you and Dad expect of me. I don't drink or take drugs. I come in when you tell me to. I've never caused you one minute of trouble, and yet you still don't trust me to make my own decisions." At that point, she lifted the record and brought it down across her knee, breaking it (try that with a CD). She dropped the pieces on the floor, then stamped back into her room. (Tom is not the only one in our family with a flair for drama.)

Kathy thought the whole thing over and made a decision. She drove to a record store, bought the same album, and brought it home. She went to Amy's room, handed her the new record, and said, "You're right. You're everything a daughter ought to be. If you think this record is all right, I'll trust your judgment."

I can imagine that some people would say this was the wrong way to go, that Kathy was backpedaling. But for Amy, nothing her mom could have done would have meant more to her. She tells me now that she actually didn't listen to the album very often, even though she still doesn't think it was as bad as Kathy feared. But she always kept the album because it was a symbol to her: her mother did trust her. The fact is, Amy has made mostly good judgments, and I now watch how fair she is with her own kids. Amy has a little bit too much of my laxness, but no one works harder for her kids— or for other people. I know how she learned to be that way.

Maybe I could have become as good a mom as Kathy if I'd stayed at the job longer than three months. But I doubt it. I stand in awe of the love Kathy has and shows to our children—and to our grandchildren.

Grandmothering

—< ✳ >—

If Kathy was a good mother, she's a *superior* grandmother. I try to keep up with her because I've had it in my mind that I would make up for all my deficiencies as a parent by being the best "Papa" ever. The truth is, though, I'm not in Kathy's league, and all the grandkids know it. Here's the giveaway: our house is called "Nana's house." I live there too, but the kids "go to Nana's house." Remember the song: "Over the river and through the woods, to Grandmother's house we go . . ." Men could complain about that, I suppose, but in our hearts we know the truth. We know whose house we live in, and we remember our own grandma's house.

My Grandpa Hughes died when I was quite young, but Grandpa Pierce was one of my favorite people in the world. He was funny and interesting, and I loved to be around him. He loved me, too. But then there were my grandmas. Grandpas love, but a lot more grandmas know how to *show* their love. They hold nothing back.

Kathy should be entering her "golden years" now, but she's actually facing one of the busiest times of her life. She's serving in the Relief Society General Presidency. So, naturally, she had to stop making pajamas and nightgowns for all her grandkids every Christmas. Right? Not right. She still does it, and she sometimes sews late into the night as Christmas approaches. She also makes an ornate cross-stitch stocking for each family member, which she hangs over our fireplace mantel. But we've been getting one or more grandchildren almost every year lately, and still she finds a way to get all that cross-stitching done, even though it takes many hours to complete.

I should say something here about Kathy and Christmas. We have a storage room approximately the size of a one-car garage that is our "Christmas storage room." Kathy collects Santa Clauses and nutcrackers, and she has many of the houses in the Dickens' Village collection. She hangs garlands from every railing and arranges her Santas and nutcrackers on every available square inch of surface in our house. I actually do help a little; I usually wire up the Dickens' Village. But you have to understand, I believe in simplicity. I want Christmas to be uncomplicated and relaxed. (Okay, I really can be lazy at times, and I've found some rhetoric to cover myself.) But Kathy transforms our house, and no wonder the kids like to come to our snowy mountain valley to see Nana's house turned into Santa's house.

And she bakes. She has about ten favorite recipes for Christmas cookies, and several for candy. (Hey, I do make the peanut brittle; remember, I like to focus on one thing and get it done.) She invariably puts in too much effort to make our Christmas nice, and at some point she gets stressed out. (Is there some natural proclivity women have toward overdoing, even when they know that's what's happening? I see so many women do the same thing.) But still, we like all the excess, with no simplicity—even though we claim every year that next year we'll go for the simplicity. I'm sure Kathy will always work way too hard, stay up too late, sew jammies, and bake her excess of love into those cookies. It's what she does.

Maybe now is a good time to tell you about the "Johanson wingding." I'm making Kathy sound way too close to perfect, and you need to know she's human. (I think we all like to know that even the best people have faults; it gives the rest of us comfort.) Kathy's mother was a Johanson from Grantsville, Utah, and according to Kathy's father, when one of the Johanson women would go ballistic, it was called a Johanson wingding. Every now and then, the kids, when they were home—usually with my able assistance—managed to push Kathy too far. She's such a pretty, gentle woman, but she could make us all cower before her righteous indignation. Many an "adjustment" came in our family when Kathy finally said, "Enough is enough." And she's a slow burner. When she gets mad, she doesn't cool off in two minutes. (I fly off the handle too, but my temper is like fireworks. There's a big pop, a brief spray of fire, and it's over.)

The great thing is, though, when it's over it's over, for both of us, and then we talk. Kathy and I have always been able to do that, and she's the same with her kids. Kathy burns for a while, but then she lets her anger go, and it's her love that we end up remembering.

The first year Kathy and I were married, she was feeling sick one Sunday morning. She asked me whether I thought she should go to church. I told her I couldn't judge that for her; she really ought to make her own decision. Kathy has since invoked that precedent as the grounds for making all her own decisions since that day. But I like that. *We* make *our* decisions. *She* makes *her* decisions. And *I* make *mine*. (Right after I check with her.)

Wait. I shouldn't say things like that. I've been facetious through most of this book, and I'd better be straight for a moment. (Kathy actually will read this book, after all.) The truth is, Kathy is a strong person, and it's one of the things I love about her. She has her own opinions and doesn't wait to see what I think before she reaches them. She's decisive and bright, and she's a great leader. She sees the big picture but also follows up on details. It's what a mother needs to be able to do, and it's why moms often make fine leaders in the family as well as outside their homes.

That stereotype we have of the mother or the grandmother wearing an apron, always ready with lots of hugs, is great, but it's only part of womanhood. Kathy loves to sew, and she bakes like crazy during the holidays, but what my kids and grandkids also know is that she's a powerhouse. She's smart, she's good, and she isn't afraid to step forward and say what she thinks.

Our family life has always been full of all the usual moments of stress and strain, along with wonderful times of togetherness, but through it all, Kathy has demonstrated to our children that women are strong. I said before that women are usually better at showing love than men are, but in saying that, let's not imply that they live only by instinct. Kathy is perceptive about other people's needs; she is unusually gracious with strangers as well as friends; and she worries about every traveler stopped in a car along the highway. But she's also analytical and curious, and she loves to learn. She's rigorously honest, and she has a strength about her that anyone who knows her has to respect—including our kids. I'm glad she's provided that example, because I want my daughter, daughters-in-law, and granddaughters to be the same way. (Who am I kidding? It's how they are already, whether I recommend it or not.)

I've worked my way, by now, into a corner. Kathy is not going to like what I've written here, and she's going to tell me to take it all out. The woman is constitutionally unable to brag, and she won't want me bragging about her. That leaves me with two choices. One is to take all that nice stuff out, and if that happens, you aren't going to be reading this paragraph, which raises one of those "tree falling in the forest" kinds of philosophical questions. The other choice is to keep her from reading the manuscript and then wait for a Johanson wingding when the book comes out. But I hope she feels what I'm trying to say: She's a remarkable woman, a great example to anyone who knows her, and especially to the generations of our family who will follow. At the same time, if I portray her as some rare jewel, I'll make the wrong point. I think she's a woman who makes the best of her good traits, but she struggles with her weaknesses, the same as anyone else. Moms and grandmothers are people, not icons, and their challenges are so big they have to settle for doing their best.

Maybe I should list a few more of Kathy's faults, just to bring her down from the stars. I accused her of raising her voice now and then, but her greater fault is that she refuses, most of the time, to speak loud enough to be heard. (I am *not* getting hard of hearing, as she claims. Just talk to her sometime; you'll be telling her to speak up too.) She forgets where she puts her keys, her cell phone, her glasses, her earrings, her purse—and a lot of other things. (I keep telling her to put things in the same place all the time, the way I do. *She's* supposed to be the one who's organized.) When I'm driving, she tells me over and over to slow down, but when I try to follow her when she's driving, I don't dare keep up with her. (She'll deny that one. And that's another fault.) She can't tell jokes very well, and she often misses the humor in really funny things other people say (which hurts, I want to tell you).

Well, okay, I'm not going to list her *real* faults. But she has them, and no one is more aware of that than she is. She often tells me that she feels like an impostor. She fears she doesn't have the skills, the wisdom, or the goodness to serve as she is serving. Is there *anyone* who doesn't feel that way at times?

All the same, she *does* have a knack for grandmothering. She remembers every birthday, does special things for the little ones on those days, and makes sure she and I get to all the special occasions. The kids probably sense that Nana is a busy person, but they also know that doesn't affect them very often. She would probably tend them a little more often were she not serving in her calling, and she wouldn't be gone as much, but she stays connected to all of them. She loves to have them come up to our house, and she thinks up all kinds of reasons to get them here. I'm all for that—with one exception. She's always inviting the kids for sleep-overs. In my mind, night is a time to enjoy red taillights, not nightlights. But Kathy likes to bring all of the cousins to our house for all-nighters, and one time she does that is at Christmastime (with everyone in their new pajamas).

The trouble is, these are young kids. Not one of them is ready to go off to a basement or up to our loft, alone. So she has bought a couple of blow-up mattresses and she gets all the kids together in the basement, and she sleeps in the middle of them. Actually, she sleeps very little, she reports. But I wouldn't know. I stay upstairs in our king-sized bed and hope that no stragglers find their way up to me. Sleep is not something I do very well, and when one of the kids is rotating in our bed (have you ever noticed how kids don't toss and turn in their sleep so much as do cartwheels?), I start looking for another place to bed down.

Kathy gets up the next morning looking bedraggled and whispering to me that she may not do that anymore, but even as she speaks, she is getting out the waffle iron. So we do waffles for the whole bunch, some of whom are still in the rub-it-all-over-their-faces-and-bodies stage, and then we start into her organized activities. When the parents show up, they're like me; they want to kick back and chat. But Kathy organizes us. We usually get pulled in slowly, whispering our complaints to each other, but we've had some wonderful fun because Kathy likes to "do something, not just sit around."

Best of all, as far as the kids are concerned, was the marshmallow war we recently fought. Kathy acquired a blueprint for a marshmallow gun made out of PVC pipe. I was skeptical that this blowgun loaded with mini-marshmallows would even work, but our older boys, not to mention their parents and I, and to some degree the little girls, all had great fun. Kathy gunned down a few bad guys herself. I spent a whole morning making those things, grumbling that it wasn't worth the time, but Kathy kept me at it and now we have an armory for future wars, and another family tradition is born. I hate to say it, but our crew would talk too much and do too little if Kathy weren't constantly pushing us toward one of her latest big ideas.

But is your family like ours? Do some of your greatest plans turn into nightmares? Our greatest disaster was actually my fault more than Kathy's, but she was the one who kept trying to convince the rest of us it was going to be great, so she took more than her share of the blame. Think about it, though: what could be greater than to take the whole family to Disney World? What could be bad about that? It sounded good to me. But there were a few things I didn't take into account.

It all started because we have a time-share in Park City, Utah, and now we've moved there—or pretty close. So we always trade our week to go somewhere else. Lately, however, we don't have much time to get away, so we had built up our trading power. We decided to go somewhere and take the family. I had some frequent-flyer miles, and Tom, who flies all the time, had a lot more. We'd go to Hawaii or the Bahamas—or somewhere great. The trouble was, July is the only month when Relief Society leaders take a breath. The other problem was, we couldn't get into any of those vacation places we wanted. So the guy helping me with the trade said, "I can get you into Orlando. You'd have a great time there."

It sounded good to me. Do I think *heat, crowds, babies?* No, I think, *I'm saved. I found a place we can go.* Even after I put the phone down, I was thinking that our kids and grandkids would be ecstatic. Kristen, who spent her mission in Florida, was the first to say, "Well, it's awfully hot and humid there in July." And gradually, others of the parents began to suggest possible problems, such as managing with six young children (that's all we had at the time) in all those crowds. But Kathy came to my defense. She promised everyone we would have a marvelous time.

As a Latter-day Saint, I'm not sure I should admit what I'm about to admit. I know there's not a single Mormon who doesn't love the Disney amusement parks, but I'm going to stand halfway up and whisper, "Not me." I'm a type-A personality. I hate lines. I'm not much on crowds either, and if I ever have to listen to one more chorus of "It's a Small World," I could crack. A thrill to me is finding out that I made a mistake in my checkbook and have a hundred dollars more than I thought I did. What I don't want is to be spun, lifted, dropped, or placed in a virtual spaceship. I only chose Disney World because I thought the grandkids would like it. But as soon as I heard the reticence of my children, I knew I had made a terrible mistake.

Not Kathy. She plowed straight ahead. It was going to be great.

Well, we went. We were in Orlando a week, and the best days were the times we traveled to the two coasts and played at the beaches. The four days in the various manifestations of Disneyism were ordeals. We thought we would run over in the mornings, when it was cool, and then, when the heat came on, return to swim in the pool at our condo. There were two things wrong with that theory. There was no cool in the morning, and it takes a full morning to get into those places. By the time we got one ride in, the kids were already frazzled. The two little girls were two, and they threw some of the most frightening tantrums I've ever experienced. The heat and the crowds and the waiting were just too much for them. The three older boys were not really old enough either. They thought they wanted to go on rides, but they would lose their nerve as they got close. The worst moment came when they all freaked out over *A Bug's Life*—the 3-D movie that features dive-bombing insects. The boys tried to believe that the things were only make-believe, but when one of the boys broke for the exit, the other two followed. (Really. I'm not making this up.)

Kathy held out. "Let's make the best of this," was her mantra. And the funny thing is, we have. First of all, the grandkids now claim to have wonderful memories of our trip to Disney World, and I think they actually do. Their parents chuckle about all the disasters: Steven waiting in line to get into the haunted house, getting in, and then screaming, "Get me out of here. I'm going to die." It's become a strangely entertaining family story—the time we suffered in Orlando for a week. The funny part is, Kathy now admits that it didn't work out, but maybe only because it's become so much fun to joke about.

It just occurred to me that we have a metaphor for life here. In some ways, life really is a long-running disaster, full of way too much stress and too many disappointments, and yet the past and future both appear precious to us. The challenge is always to survive the present. To do that, we need someone like the coxswain on an eight-person crew, calling out the pace, telling us we can do it. I like that picture. It's a good image for a mother. (And notice, there are no aprons, no cookies.)

By the way, I did have one wonderful experience in Orlando. I kept the two little girls at the condo one day, and we played Polly Pockets (I was the only one who could change the rubber clothes on those little dolls), and we colored and played games, went for a walk, and read books. I was a mother again, and it wasn't chaotic. It was lovely, and the girls were peaceful (they didn't even fight with each other), and best of all, we didn't have to be at MGM Studios, or wherever it was the others went that day.

Part of being good grandparents is staying involved, I think, and I'm afraid I would drift into peacefulness and seclusion if Kathy weren't pulling me into another one of her schemes to "get us all together." (At least I've won out on avoiding campouts, which our kids organize. Kathy can live without ever sleeping in a bag again, as can I.) But it's interesting what Kathy tells me about wanting to gather our clan. She says that she likes to be with the kids because she wants to get grandmothering right. She has regrets about her mothering. (Maybe that *is* a universal feeling.) She tells me that she wishes now that she had been a little more at ease with our kids. (Hey, wasn't that what I was trying to help her do?) She says, "I wish I had just loved them more."

Sometimes, Kathy now feels, she worked hard at meeting the

needs of our kids and making sure they got taught all the right things, but she didn't take enough time to enjoy them. With her grandchildren, she wants to do things a little differently. What she does so well is accept these little kids who are noisier than any eight kids ought to be, who have their little fears and phobias, and who really are delicate in some ways—and simply love them. She doesn't need a reason, and the kids know they don't have to "earn" Grandma's love.

That's a grandma's job, and let me say to all grandpas who might be listening in, it's our job too. And it's a good one. I delight in our grandchildren much more unabashedly than I ever did my own kids. Even when they're bad, they make me laugh. Our little Billy is a wonderfully good-natured boy, with a smile that excuses his habit of getting into everything. I watch Rob, who wants to be such a good dad, and I see him reprimanding little Billy, teaching him what the limits are. For punishment, when Billy gets out of hand on his search-and-destroy missions, Rob and Stacy sometimes have him stand with his nose to the wall. I watch, and I try not to smile, but it's so funny when Billy goes right back to his work, not long after he's released from his "time out." Of course, the reason I laugh is that I'm thinking of Robert at that age. I think to myself, Rob is right. He needs to teach his son. But Kathy is right, too; we really should take more pleasure in our kids during those years they are with us.

Kathy now says that the thing she didn't know when she was a young mother was that time would pass so quickly. She and I watch our daughter and daughters-in-law with their little ones, and we know what they go through at times, and how long the days and months can seem as they wait for their kids to be "out of diapers" or "in school" or "able to dress themselves." But one day those kids will be leaving home, and then their parents will wonder why they wished the years away. We all do it. Kathy did it. But now she wishes she hadn't, and she's not going to wish these years away. She's going to have the joy with her grandchildren that she sometimes didn't relish as a young mother.

My Mom

— ❖ —

In some ways my mom was a terrible example for other mothers. When I was a teenager, I would wear a shirt, throw it on a chair, or even drop it on the floor, and by the next day the shirt had disappeared. But it wasn't in the Friday box. It was hanging in my closet. It had already been washed, starched, ironed, and made available for my next opportunity to choose it from the others that she had taken care of the same way. No wonder I'm not a better person than I am. My mom pampered me. She indulged me. If she had ever read a book on mothering, she would have known better. And in all honesty, it's too bad she didn't, because Dad and my brothers and I really did take advantage of her. But I've never been able to work up much resentment against her. I'll just try to live with the bad traits I probably learned from her spoiling me.

I can't resist an "aside" at this point. When Kathy and I got married, I started off the same way. I would wear a shirt once and toss it in the hamper, or even leave it on a chair in our bedroom. Kathy was teaching at that time, and I was in college full-time and working part-time. Before long, a big supply of shirts began building up in our hamper. One Saturday Kathy decided to catch up on "her" ironing. After all, I didn't know how to iron; that was "women's work." It had never occurred to me that a man could iron, should iron, or that some other system existed besides wear it, drop it, and get it back in good repair. Kathy, at the same time, was trying to be a good wife, and the honeymoon wasn't really over.

So Kathy started in on my shirts, and I'm not sure what I was doing—studying or whatever. And then along comes a close friend who tells me he really needs to talk to me for a few minutes. I told Kathy that I was going to take a short drive with my friend and would be back before long. So off we went. But my friend, who was still single, was having concerns over his love life, and being the sensitive guy I am, I listened to his whole story, and being an experienced married man, I gave him a lot of advice.

Actually, I'm not exactly sure it went that way, but I do remember we talked over his concerns. Well, all that took a while. Kathy remembers that I was gone all afternoon. As best I recall it was only a couple of hours, but either way, it was *way too long*. When I got back to our apartment, I didn't have to ask whether Kathy was upset.

I don't think we argued. As I recall, Kathy told me what she thought of the idea of ironing a dozen shirts or more while I was out for a drive with my friend. But here's the interesting thing about that. I saw the justice of her claims immediately. (Once again, that's how I remember it; Kathy may have a different version to tell.) She was right and I was wrong. She didn't mind ironing as long as I was going to carry my share of the load, but she wasn't going to work while I played.

I can iron a little now. But I don't iron much. In fact, I'm always trying to convince Kathy that she irons way too many things that don't need ironing. I sit at my computer most of my life, and I like natural-fiber shirts that learn the contours (and flab) of my body. They don't need to be stiffened. Kathy, on the other hand, irons my stay-pressed Dockers. They really don't need it, from my point of view, but she says they don't look their best without pressing.

But . . . while Kathy irons, I am often found cleaning a bath-room, vacuuming the living room, or sweeping the kitchen. Over the years, as our lives have changed in various ways, we have readjusted our "chore assignment," but we have always tried to make the load fair (without the chore wheel). Since Kathy is "at work" most days with her church calling and I do my work at home, when she calls home to say she's on her way from Salt Lake, I often start dinner. (The good news is, I cook; the bad news is, I don't cook well. Mostly I defrost things that start out frozen, and I put already cut-up salad ingredients on a plate, or I open soup cans and heat the contents. Nonetheless, we have something ready to eat when Kathy gets home.)

But what does this have to do with my mother? More than might seem obvious. Maybe Mom didn't make me take care of my own shirts, and maybe I did way too little around our house, but what Mom brought to our family was the commitment that she would always do her part willingly.

Mom was way too close to a servant to my dad, but marriages tended to be like that in those days. Men didn't do "housework." The world has changed, and the balance has had to adjust. Isn't it interesting that when a woman does housework, it's "cleaning" or whatever; when a man does housework, he's "helping." Notice, too, that when women are home with their children, they're home with their children. When men stay home, they're "baby-sitting." Maybe we haven't changed our thinking quite enough.

So my mom didn't ever announce to Dad that she wasn't going to iron his shirts unless he shared in the work around the house. It took a younger, stronger woman to make that stand with me. But Mom taught me about a willing heart (and so has Kathy). Mom gave her full effort in our family, and that was my image of what a married person should do.

My mother's situation was not easy. Dad was a good man, but he made things difficult for Mom. She was devoted to the Church—worked in Primary in our ward and stake for thirty-eight years—and she wanted her kids to grow up believing. Dad rarely went to church. He also had his weaknesses, alcohol being the most serious. Still, Dad worked hard all his life, showed up every day at a job he didn't like most of those years, and he always provided for us. He was proud of his sons, too, and supported us in the things we did. He followed us around as we got involved in athletics and other activities, and he spent most of what he made on us—even though he never did make much.

Dad had to quit school after eighth grade, and he didn't read very well. He was actually interested in his world and always concerned about current events, so we talked a lot about ideas in our home, but Dad was raised in a time when fathers were not likely to be as involved with their kids as they are now, and he didn't know how to *tell* us he was proud of us or that he loved us. He never said anything to me like that—not once. He tried many times to give up drinking, but he would always go back to it. He mainly drank on weekends, but when he did, he changed. He could be mean then—not physically abusive, but verbally, especially to Mom.

My only reason to bring all this up is to say that my mother led a lonely life at times. Dad tended to withdraw to his garage where he tinkered with his cars and lawn mowers, and he also withdrew, over time, more and more into his alcoholism. Every now and then he would explode with unwarranted anger and accuse my mom of all kinds of things that his drunken mind conjured up. Those were terrifying times for me. Maybe Mom shouldn't have taken all that. Maybe she should have sought a divorce. Most women, especially now, would. And maybe part of the reason she didn't was that she had no resources of her own, no way to provide for us. But I don't think she thought about that. She was married and she had three kids, and she was going to make the best of it. Dad could be a great guy, and he was much of the time, so she chose to live with her situation. That may not have been the right decision, but it was the one she made.

But she did more than that. She always talked to me about Dad, and her theme was that I should be patient and understanding of him. He had his faults, but he was a good man, a hard worker. She wanted me to be proud of him. He eventually worked at Hill Air Force Base as a civilian sheet metal worker. But earlier, he was a "body and fender man," as "collision repairmen" were called back then. She would tell me what an amazing artist he was at fixing and painting crashed cars so they looked like new.

At a fairly young age, I began to be ashamed of my father. After all, we lived in Ogden, a mostly Mormon town at that time, and I had a father who drank and smoked and swore and didn't go to church. I didn't know what to say when other boys asked why my dad did those things. But Mom would tell me that he had bad habits he wanted to break—and he *was* someone I could believe in. And then she would tell me what a master he was at fixing cars. I know that she sensed how much I wanted a reason to have faith in my own father.

And here's the thing: she believed it. She believed he had bad habits but that he could be good, and she believed he had his skills. As a teenager I came to doubt all that, and there were times, after Dad would treat me with a harshness that seemed way beyond necessary, that I wanted to hate the man. I saw so little generosity in him, so little kindness, and I hated what he did to Mom on those occasions when he let the alcohol rule his mind. But Mom would just keep pleading with me to think the best of him, to remember what he had done for us, how hard he worked, and all the rest.

Dad and I fought when I first discovered that I knew everything—at about age fifteen. What surprises me now is that I've stayed pretty close to his political leanings, and I have more of him in me than I like to admit. I respect him for his struggle now, how hard he worked in spite of his distaste for what he did each day, and how he stuck with his job as a father even when other forces were pulling him in bad directions. What I think of now is how carefully he cared for his yard, and especially his roses. I've been a raiser of roses myself, since then, and I understand the love. I tell myself now that Dad felt affection for things and didn't know what to do about those feelings. But I know it was Mom, always saying, "He *is* a good man, at heart, Dean," that kept me trying to believe in him.

What I didn't know then, and recognize now, is what a trial my mother's own life was. She received so little tenderness from Dad, at least that I ever saw, and she had to carry on her religious life by herself. She had no sister and no daughters, so she turned to the sisters in our ward and found people she could talk to. And she turned to her sons. I talked with Mom about everything, and that has changed my life. I was eating dinner at a gathering of a hundred people or so one time, and a woman turned to me and said, "Do you realize you're the only man in this room?" I looked around and saw that she was right. "I guess I am," I told her. "I hadn't thought about it." And then she said something surprising to me: "You like women, don't you?"

I realized she was right. I've always been verbal, and I do express my emotions, and that's supposed to be more of a female thing. But I learned it from my mother. I learned that it was good to talk out my worries by sharing them with someone who cared. And I listened to her worries. She didn't bad-mouth Dad, but she would talk about her frustrations and her wishes. I suspect that her sisters in the Church—the women she went to Relief Society with and worked in Primary and Young Women with—heard more about her difficulties, and I don't know what she would have done without the Church, but she taught me that it was okay to express my feelings and share my concerns. I've tried to be that way with my own kids, and I think I've done fairly well. They've always had Kathy to talk to as well, but I don't think our kids have hesitated to talk to me. All children have things they don't say to their parents, and no doubt that's true for my kids, but we've had lots of good, open conversations, and I don't know whether they know, but that's definitely something passed along to them from my mother.

My mother had trouble carrying babies. She had a number of miscarriages in fairly advanced pregnancies. One of the babies she lost was mature enough to identify as a girl. But she never had that girl. She wanted to name her daughter Diane, so when I was born, she gave me the closest name to Diane she could think of. (Also, my little brother's middle name is Duane.) But because of the miscarriages, my brothers and I are spread out. I'm four and a half years younger than my older brother, and my little brother is almost ten years younger than I. In some ways, I think we were each raised separately, and Mom never had that girl she could share things with. She loved to sew, to can fruit, to do crafts, and she had no daughter to teach those things, but maybe the benefit that came to us boys was that she shared so much of herself with us. It hurts me now to think how sad her life must have been much of the time, but she never said that. She was upbeat, optimistic, busy, and absolutely

certain that her sons were great young men, destined to do wonderful things with their lives.

Some people have wondered how I ended up a writer. After all,
I was raised in what people would now call poverty. My first home
was a trailer house. It was eight feet wide and sixteen feet long.
Travel trailers are much bigger. This was a tiny thing my dad built,
parked between Grant and Lincoln Avenues in Ogden. If you know
that area, you know this was not a "prestige" property. We had no
running water. Our bathroom was in the washhouse, maybe fifty
feet away, and we kept our food in an icebox outside. We had a coal
stove, and my brother and I bathed in a galvanized tub, heated with
water off that stove. We kept our drinking water in a bucket. I lived
there until I was five and my brother was nine, and then we moved
into an old house that had been divided into apartments, but we
shared a bathroom with another family. Eventually we moved into a
little house on Grant Avenue, one my parents saved to buy while
they lived so simply. The house cost $5,800.

When I was little I didn't think of myself as poor, but we were,
in some sense of that word. By the time I was in high school, I
acquired some shame at living in the wrong part of town, but over-
all, we were more secure than most families because we didn't buy
what we couldn't afford. But the point is, my father could barely
read, and I would have been designated "at-risk" by current stan-
dards, and yet I became an English teacher and a writer. Perhaps
that's because what we did at night in that little trailer was listen to
the books that Mom would read to us. I sometimes think, now, it's
the kids with TV and a dozen other electronic devices who are at

risk. We had a radio, which only came into clear focus if your imagination was tuned, and we had my mother to read stories to us. (We also had a library not far away, and I started going there early—because my mom taught me to love books.)

My mother's three sons became her universe, and she was our universe, too, in many ways. We grew up and did all the things other kids did, but she was our anchor. She was the one who believed in us when we made mistakes, failed, or did well. To this day—and my mother died more than a decade ago—I can never have something good happen to me without thinking, "I wish I could call Mom. She'd love to hear this."

I've talked about Kathy and her devotion to making Christmas nice. My mom was the same way, but she didn't have the resources to do much. She decorated the tree with those ugly "icicles" that were popular in those days, and she had a wreath for the door and a few other things to put out around the house. One year she went on one of those kicks that Relief Society sisters used to get on, and she made some elaborate candles that were covered with some sort of foaming wax. They looked like Salt Lake's "This Is the Place Monument" in design and were almost as big. She dyed them into various colors, but my own recollection is that they were not things of great beauty. Of course, maybe I only think of them that way because she would put hers away after Christmas each year and haul them out the next year, and I think they got a little banged up over time (and certainly, dated).

It tugs at me still, however, to think how hard she tried. And Dad really never got into any of that. I don't remember him ever helping to decorate the tree, and he didn't buy presents, not even for Mom. I think he saw Christmas as a big expense, and money was always a concern for us. Mom knew all that, and so every fall she would work for a few weeks to earn money so she could give her family a nice Christmas.

There were two ways Mom could earn money. She worked at a plant that made ketchup. She called it "working in the tomatoes." She would stand at a conveyor belt and peel the tomatoes, then toss them into a container. I never saw her do that; I only heard about it. Her other means of income was to work for my uncle, her brother, who was a builder. She would clean new houses when they were finished and ready for someone to move into. She did that at various times during the year, but the money was always for us— for Christmas or birthdays or other special times. When I graduated from high school, she used "her" money to buy me a suit, and she saved Gold-Strike Stamps, which were the big thing then, to buy me a watch.

Lots of moms do things like that. But there's a "rest of the story" in Mom's case. If you were to talk to someone now whose hands went numb at night and were stiff and miserably sore, you would know what caused her problems: carpal tunnel syndrome. But at that time, there was no operation, and no one seemed to know what the problem was. Mom suffered with it all her life. She couldn't hold a telephone receiver without her hands going numb, so she would shift the receiver from one hand to the other, over and over, as she talked. So what work did she do? Peeling tomatoes and cleaning the paint off windows with a razor blade and other such jobs around those new houses. Nothing is more difficult for someone with carpal tunnel than repetitive acts that involve gripping.

I can remember my mother getting up in the morning with her hands doubled together as though she had arthritis. But she would drive out to the ketchup place and peel tomatoes all day. She would tell us that after she worked for a while, her hands would loosen up and weren't so bad. What I didn't fully realize at the time was that the pain comes mostly at night. I know this now, because I've had surgery on both of my hands to rid them of my carpal tunnel problems, but she never had that option available and still went back "to the tomatoes" every fall, knowing what it would do to her—all so we could have a nice Christmas.

One of the warmest experiences of my life occurred one Christmas when I was about sixteen. I mentioned that my dad didn't buy presents, but one year, a couple of days before Christmas, he got out his wallet, handed me a twenty-dollar bill, and said, "Why don't you go find something for your mom." My dad would have had no idea what to buy, but I was sure I could do it, so I went downtown, looked in some windows, and then ended up where I knew I would have to go: J. C. Penney's. I wanted to buy a dress for my mother—a church dress. Only in Penney's would I have a chance of finding something for twenty dollars.

I remember looking through the racks of dresses and getting confused and embarrassed as the "ladies" in the women's department glanced at me. Finally a nice clerk came up and asked to help. I don't know whether I knew Mom's size or not. She was a short little woman, not much over five feet, and by that time she was rather plump. I either described my mom or I got her size from one of her dresses. In any case, the clerk guided me to the right rack and I looked at beautiful dresses that, even in 1958, were all over twenty dollars. I finally found a navy blue dress in a sort of crepe fabric, I think you would call it. As I remember, it had a white collar. I only know I thought it was beautiful, and the clerk told me I could get it for twenty dollars. I eventually decided that the woman wanted me to have the dress so badly that she either paid for part of it herself, or she created her own "sale price." I don't know if that's the case, but I wrote a short story later where that's what happened, and the story sometimes takes the place of reality in my mind. In the story, I bought the dress at L. R. Samuels, but that's only because I wanted to buy it in that beautiful store where the wealthy women of Ogden shopped.

In any case, I bought it at Penney's, and I could hardly stand to wait for Christmas morning. When Mom opened the package, she knew immediately that Dad hadn't bought it and she guessed that I had done it—which made me immensely proud. She tried it on and it fit, and she *loved* it. She wore that dress until it must have fallen apart. And she would always tell everyone, "This is the dress Dean picked out for me." I think because of that I've always loved to shop for my wife. I suspect that I have wonderful taste. I've made some bad choices sometimes, and occasionally Kathy has returned my purchases, but I've hit some real home runs, too, usually because I have a little more range of purchasing power now, but I think I'm always trying to re-create that moment when Mom pulled that dress out of the package and responded with joy that she could own something so beautiful—bought at Penney's.

I wish I could buy her something now. Kathy and I once bought her a dryer because she had gone all her life without one, and that was nice, but that navy blue dress—I can't even think of it without tears filling my eyes. She had always had so little, and she gave us boys so much.

But before I start weeping too much, I need to pull back right at this point and make something clear. I've never liked most of the talks I hear in church on Mother's Day, and I'm sounding a little too much like that right now. Here's the Mother's Day logic I hate. We say, "My mother is always self-sacrificing; she takes the smallest piece of pie and she never looks out for herself because she does everything for us. She cleans and scrubs and picks up after us and works her fingers to the bone, and I appreciate it." We ought to follow that line of thought with the right conclusion: "But I'm going to change all that because it really isn't right. I'm going to take a smaller piece of pie myself from now on. And I'm going to scrub the tub and the toilets and pick up after *myself*."

It's as though we think we can thank a mother once a year and then send her back to the salt mines. The artistry of that approach is, we shame her into being a great self-sacrificer by describing this perfect person she knows darned well she isn't. I've heard many women say that they don't like Mother's Day because they hear *ad nauseam* about Mrs. Perfect, and then they go home and feel painfully inadequate.

What I wish is that I had realized a whole lot sooner that Mom was a sort of slave in our home. I wish I had perceived her pain and loneliness and worried less about me and more about her. I wish I'd learned to iron or scrub a toilet or do something useful that would have taken some of the weight off her shoulders. And I will say this: once Kathy and I had kids who were old enough, our family cleaned the house together every Saturday morning. My sons, just as well as my daughter, can clean a bathroom and make it shine, and they may have grumbled about being organized by the chore chart, but we all did work together to take care of the house and yard.

It's not wrong to praise my mom for her willingness to serve her family at a cost to herself, but on the other hand, I praise my wife for standing up for fairness. My mother should have stood up for herself a whole lot more. Still, what I said in the beginning was that I never doubted that her life was a devotion to her family, and I see the same thing in Kathy's life, even though she is much busier than my mom ever was. What I think that kind of devotion can inspire is a desire on husbands' and children's parts to return the same devotion. Too many men see their careers as first in their lives, and their families as second. We now see more and more women taking on the same attitude, we criticize them, but I think that all of us, of both sexes, should listen to what our leaders have always taught us: our family is our first responsibility.

When I got home from my mission, after two and a half years in Germany, I walked in from the airplane and my mom grabbed me and hugged me. My dad reached out and shook my hand. I've been wondering ever since what he might have done if I had pulled him into my arms. I know he would have gone stiff as a pole—but I wish I had done it. I didn't know how to embrace him any more than he knew how to embrace me. I made up my mind when Kathy and I had kids that I wouldn't be like that. I would kiss and hug any sons I had, as well as daughters. And I have done that. Whatever I know about love, I learned mostly from my mother, and I hope it's in our family to stay. But I hope I'm also giving my all to my marriage and my family, as my mother did. Sons should learn to do that, the same as daughters.

Wisdom of a One-Time Mother

—⟨ ✳ ⟩—

What did I learn by trying out motherhood? Not enough to start giving advice to women who don't have short-term contracts, as I did. But I honestly believe that no other job on this planet is quite as big or important. I could make a case that a head of state, like the U.S. president, has a bigger job, and certainly a crucial one, but presidents have Camp David, a ranch to escape to, golf—or something. A mother's job is relentless. It never goes away, not even at night. Certainly not at night. Every mother learns to sleep with one eye sort of half open. And she gets no sick leave. It's usually easier to plow ahead than to take a chance on what might happen in the house if she stays in bed a day or two.

I hope I'm not coming across as condescending. Moms hear too much of that kind of stuff: "Really, you're the important ones. We men go out and kill the dragons, but you women get to rock the cradle, and honest, that's more important." The fact is, men think

up way too many dragons, and the other fact is, there are no dragons. The time and energy men put into their competitions, whether
in the business world or at football games, is sometimes
laughable—at least in terms of how seriously we tend to take ourselves. Making a living is important, but creating a life and sustain-
ing it is in another realm. It seems to me that men ought to say, "I'm
sorry, honey, I have to run off and make a little money, but I'll get
back home to the important stuff as soon as I can."

I don't want to play down the importance of a good and noble
father. He can, if he will, guide a family in righteousness, along with
his wife. He can and should be a spiritual leader in his home. I sit in
priesthood meeting with great men who grasp the fullness of the
gospel and are striving in every way they can to fill all the roles
required of them. And yet, far too often, as President Gordon B.
Hinckley keeps reminding us, men are the ones who let their
families down. (If any men are sneaking a peek at this book, let me
ask you a question. How often do you come home and say something like, "Sweetheart, kids, it's Monday, as you know, so tonight
is family home evening. I spent some time on Sunday preparing a
lesson and I have a nice activity planned. It's going to be swell." Or
is it more likely that your wife reminds you that it's Monday night,
and *she* has prepared [or no one has], and somewhere deep in the
cortex of your testosterone-drenched brain, a nasty thought arises:
"But it's Monday Night Football tonight.")

God is our father. Christ is both a father to us and a brother. But
isn't it interesting that when Christ appeared to the Nephites in the
new world, he used a female image to describe himself: "How oft

have I gathered you as a hen gathereth her chickens under her wings, and have nourished you" (3 Nephi 10:4). It's also interesting that when we describe the traits of Christ, we use words like meek, humble, gentle, gracious, and loving. But most of these terms, in our society, we associate more with women than with men, and we sometimes, even today, see such qualities as evidence of male weakness. But women need strength and men need tenderness for the best child raising.

We've all seen every kind of parent do well with children, and we've seen seemingly perfect parents run into trouble. Part of that is the agency of the child. But I still think mothers worry too much about being perfect technicians every day of their lives. I've laughed a lot about the craziness of raising kids, but I recognize it's not all funny. Far too many women are having serious struggles with depression. Kathy went through a postpartum depression that developed into panic attacks and debilitating obsessive thoughts that plagued her for more than a year, so I know very well that the challenges women face can't always be laughed away (even though humor *can* be the best help at times). Mothers need time for themselves, and they need to draw on the powers that can give them strength. It may be more important for women to *make* time—even *expect* husbands and children to arrange time—to devote to their spiritual growth than to fuss about whether they are right about every decision they make.

Kathy experienced a terrible moment when Rob was little. He was eating a peanut-butter sandwich and choked on it. She tried everything to dislodge the blockage, reaching a finger into his throat and pounding on his back, but nothing worked. He was turning blue, and Kathy panicked. She grabbed him and ran outside with him. She wasn't even sure where she was going, but she knew she needed help. As she ran toward a neighbor's house, the bouncing must have had the right effect. Suddenly Robert was gasping and getting air. She worried afterward that she had done all the wrong things, and yet her will to save her child had been absolute. Her decision was perhaps not the best one, but it worked, more or less by accident. Or God was with her and knew the purity of her heart. Parents do their best, and they often do it wrong, but their commitment and will is certainly as important as their methods.

It's always seemed to me that kids need, as much as anything, to feel that their parents are "on their side." Kids need to feel that the ultimate goal their parents have is to do the best they can for them, not merely satisfy some inner need for control. And that's not always easy to keep straight in our own heads. Kathy and I had a couple of parenting theories that sometimes became difficult to make work. One of those was a belief that it was better for our kids not to work part-time while they were going to school. The idea was that they ought to get summer jobs to do their part and to learn to work, but during the school year their job was to do well in their studies—and to *earn scholarships*. We figured they would make more money, in the long run, that way. We also didn't think that high-schoolers needed their own cars. (One of the reasons young people want to work is so they can have those cars.) But that meant that we had to juggle two cars among us, and that got complicated.

Then a test of our theory came up. Rob was a good student, and as part of his own educational plan, he really wanted to take an advanced placement class in political science. His high school didn't offer one, but the other high school in Provo did. Rob could travel across town and take the class at about one o'clock every day, but for that he needed a car. I could let him take mine some days, since I worked at home, but I often needed a car during the day. I knew how much Rob wanted this, so I offered to pick him up, take him over, and then go get him again at the end of the class. That meant a short drive to his high school, and maybe ten minutes to the other school—no big deal. The trouble was, in less than an hour I had to be back. I made it work as best I could, and yet it was always awkward. *But,* Rob and I had some great talks in those ten-minute drives, about politics and all kinds of things, *and* I think it was a way to say to him, "I'm with you. I'll help you do the good things you want to do."

I have no idea whether Rob thought it was a big deal then, or whether he does now. But to me, it was my way of telling him how much I loved him, how much I appreciated his intellectual curiosity, and how pleased I was that he was making good choices. No doubt, a parent can indulge children way too much, but again, I strongly believe our kids have to know that we're trying our best to support them.

One of our problems is that we worry too much about what other people think of our parenting skills. Even as we're asking not to be judged by others, we do too much judging ourselves. Mothers too often compare each of the best qualities of other women against their own worst traits. So one friend is really fit, and one keeps wonderful scrapbooks, and another has an ultra-clean house. "What's wrong with me? Why can't I do that?" moms ask themselves, not stopping to think that the same women have weaknesses as well, and not remembering personal skills that make other women jealous.

Before we have children, we think most of the parents sitting in sacrament meeting ought to "do something about their kids." Once we have kids, we think everyone ought to be a lot more understanding about what we're trying to survive during the meeting. And once our kids are grown, we think, "I never let my kids get away with that." We really all need to chill out. Kathy is wonderful about being the grandma who reaches over the bench and takes a baby from a mom. She doesn't criticize the overwhelmed mother; she helps her. And she loves to hold the baby, too.

Kristen, my daughter-in-law, was attending her book-club meeting and had no choice but to take her crawling baby with her. He pulled himself up to a coffee table and before she could stop him, he lashed out with one arm and swept all the goodies and drinks onto the floor. Things crashed in all directions—and all over the carpet. A few minutes later, Kris discovered that Tal had "blown out" a diaper, dropping solid waste all over himself, her, and the same carpet. What was Kris worried about? She told me she was humiliated, and the thought that came to her mind was, "What will these women think of me?" As if a woman doesn't have a big enough job, all too often she feels she has to wonder what her parents and in-laws think of her parenting skills, as well as her husband who comes home to explain how she really ought to handle things, and then she worries about every other mother she knows and how much better job they're doing than she is.

Of all the people who understand one another, mothers ought to lead the way. Unfortunately, that's often not the case. Young mothers try to polish up their kids for church (while their husbands are out doing church work, as often as not), and then feel a little sick inside because "Sister Smithers'" kids look nicer than their own. But we really all ought to back off on that kind of stuff. Once we meet the perfect mother—who really only raises her dreadful head in Mother's Day talks—we should enshrine her, build a statue to the Unknown Mother, and then admit that she's the only example of perfection who will ever exist. We could maybe give out little statues of her at Mother's Day sacrament meetings, made out of chocolate, and then the mothers could take her home and bite her head off—and get a nice little chocolate rush at the same time.

Maybe the hardest thing about mothering is keeping a clear picture, amid the confusion, of what the goal is. Tal's name is really Taliesin—not exactly one of the fad names of our time. But it was the name of a young Welshman who was Tal's third-great-grandfather. He joined the Church with his family and, after his mother died in giving birth, he ended up at sixteen, with a seventeen-year-old sister, playing a major role in raising their siblings—a heavy responsibility for one so young. It's an extreme example of a little trick mortality plays on us. When we are young, we think primarily of ourselves growing up. We dream our dreams and set our goals. But just at the age when we come into our own, we often become parents. And suddenly, life is not so much about "us" as we always thought it was going to be. Our parents had to do the same thing. Not long after they left their parents' homes, they had to give up some of that self they were searching for—and put their children first. It happens over and over, and we all owe to our children what we got from our parents.

Tal has inherited everything we believe as a family, and it all came down from old Grandpa Taliesin Hughes, whom not one of us ever knew. But we owe him something, and Tom and Kris gave their son his name. It represents a commitment to pass on to the next generation what we've received. And that's more important than we are.

I now know what I did wrong the summer I was home with my kids. I did the job each day, but deep down I wanted to be doing something else, something more important to me. In my case, it was to build my knowledge so that I would be ready for my classes that fall. My first priority was my career, I hate to admit. Taking care of kids, to me, was like sitting in an airport waiting for my flight to come in. It was time to kill while waiting to get on with my trip. What I fear is that our world has made mothers feel the same way. I don't think there's anything wrong with looking forward to a time when personal goals can take higher priority again, but no mom should have to apologize for giving her kids her full attention. That doesn't mean canceling all thoughts of self, but it usually means putting a lot of things on the back burner for a while and knowing that the job is worth the work. Life has seasons: a time will come when the learning that derives from those intense years of child care will join with native gifts, and there will be time for other personal goals.

So, do all mother's go to heaven? I guess it depends on what we mean by heaven. We can all look forward to another life after this one—even dads. But will all moms be exalted? Not really. We all know there are some terrible mothers around—women who abandon their children, abuse them, or indulge their own needs with little thought of the effect their selfishness has on their kids. We see the mess that comes from parents who don't care enough. But I like what Amy told me. She had been listening to the rebroadcast of a talk that Elder Neal A. Maxwell had given at BYU years ago. He spoke of church lessons and scripture study as the education we receive, and of life as our laboratory. Amy liked that thought and she added to it. She told me, "I really think that being a mother is the ultimate lab experience, even though sometimes it seems like the test is just too great." And then she used a word I've used in this book. She said that the job is "relentless." But she was trying to encourage herself, and so she said, "The thing is, I can't imagine any woman getting through it and not becoming a better person. Everything about being a mother demands the best of you."

Some mothers might actually wonder what Amy was fussing about. I know mothers who are like the eye in the middle of the storm—serene and confident and untroubled. Some seem to do mothering naturally, and they probably ask themselves why others struggle so hard. Still, I know few mothers who don't find plenty of exasperation in keeping up with the multiplicity, intensity, and emotional drain that is inherent in the work. Thinking of what Amy said, though, it seems to me there's a reason that men look at their wives and wonder how they have managed to rise to a higher level. We make our bold attempts, and we give our sermons, and we try to walk the walk, but more often than not, women have a deeper resource of love and patience and goodness.

All mothers aren't headed for heaven. But what about yours? There's not one doubt in my mind about my mother. And don't almost all of us feel that way? I think the most honored name in the world is "Mother," and we usually compare ours, as Lincoln did, to an angel. The fact is, our moms are human, and they mess up, and their best isn't perfect, but she's still "Mom." Anyone who has the title should cherish it.

I've mentioned our little grandson, Samuel. At seven months, he has perfected a surprising talent. Most kids pull themselves up to things at that age, and sometimes they'll let go and balance for a moment. But Sam can actually crawl, stop, and then get up to his feet without touching anything. He spreads his legs unusually wide, and that seems to help him find his balance. But after getting up, he still doesn't dare take a step. I doubt he could, with his legs so far apart. All the same, he's very proud of himself, and when he gets up that way, he'll wave his arms and roar. It's as though he's saying, "Hey, everybody, look at me. I can stand up like the rest of you." You can tell he's just busting to make it to that next level, as all kids are. And moms, we owe it to these children to help them get there. Someone, after all, helped us. I like to picture little Samuel, when he stands like that, as a little Samuel the Lamanite, raising his voice in the name of all that is good. What I suspect is that ol' Samuel the

Lamanite must have had a pretty good mother—and a good dad—and yet, at two, he probably gave his parents fits.

When I was maybe six, a boy threw a rock at me and hit me in the head. When I touched my hair and felt blood, I knew what I had to do; I took off running for home. Mom would take care of me. By the time I reached my house, blood was running down my neck and soaking into my shirt. I threw open the door and ran inside—where I would be okay. I can still remember the look of utter shock I saw on my mother's face and the sense I had immediately that she didn't know what to do. It was a terrifying moment. If she didn't know, who did? But she cleaned me up and bandaged me as best she knew how, and I healed all right. That's all a mom can do. Mothers would like to be experts in a thousand specialties, but they're not. I know all about that. When I was a mother, my kids were not really in very good hands. I'm amazed they trusted me. But that's what kids do. They make the best of what they've got.

That's what God does, too. He makes the best of his daughters by trusting them with others of *his* children. Her job doesn't guarantee that she'll get home to him, but it's certainly some of the best on-the-job training a mortal can receive.